Silent Tears, Poems
and other Stories

Written by

Stephen J George

*Gerald
with best wishes
Stephen George
Dec 2014*

Silent Tears, Poems and other Stories

ISBN: 978-1-910181-07-2

Published December 2014

Illustrations by Stephen George

Printing in Great Britain by Anchorprint Group Limited, Leicester
www. anchorprint.co.uk

Published by Clouds Associates in conjunction with Anchor Print Ltd.

Other Books by Stephen George

Free Spirit - A Nomadic Story

Western Adventure

Acknowledgements

Like a thunderstorm one needs a trigger action to create an event; that was when Helen Clough introduced me to a diary from the Second World War. It was written by a person who was trapped in London. From that beginning I spoke to Sylvia Bondsfield, Dot Flynn, Patricia Whiteside, Christine Vanderweele and John Holden and Nurse Phyllis Hinsley.
They were the inspiration to Silent Tears.

Helen Clough is a librarian with the Open University

I am indebted to Lynne Gray and Norma Ashley for reading the manuscripts and to my constant advisor and Editor Julia Arkell.

Richard George read all the stories and helped the set up and organisation of this book, without his IT skills the book would still be a manuscript.

Stephen George

Trusthorpe October 2014

Silent Tears, Poems and other Stories

Contents

All the stories have facts and truths, you my reader will have to seek the wheat from the chaff.

SILENT TEARS

A Short Story

by

Stephen George

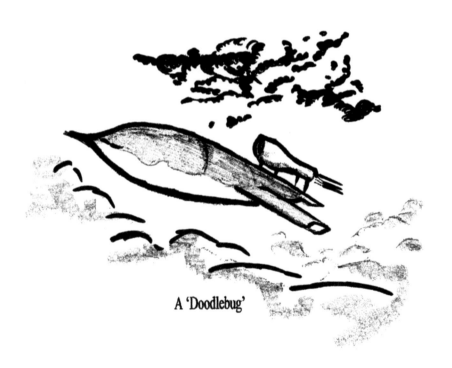

A 'Doodlebug'

Children from Silent Tears

Dot Flynn

John Hudson

Pat Whiteside

Sylvia Bondsfield

SILENT TEARS

It was 1940; the Guard slammed the door, blew his whistle and waved his green flag, the steam blasted up between the engine and platform. The train, filled with children shivering like frightened mice, dragged its way from the grey-black smoking buildings. Another night of the London Blitz; the Luftwaffe had pounded the capital again. The children slumped deeply into their seats; heavy hearted, they could not imagine a future.

*   *   *

Their glasses clinked, sitting in a pub in Northampton, the memories came dribbling back. The three pensioners had been invited to a reunion by Phyllis. She was loved by all. She had a passion for the welfare of older people and admired these survivors of the Blitz.

'Well where shall we start? I really want to know how you solved the mystery and who was given the reward; you were given a reward for all your efforts?'

Phyllis was visibly excited now. She was hoping they would recall those days when they were inseparable friends; none were related but had been bonded by strong ties developed in a time of crisis. Jack's glass shook as he lifted it to his thin crinkled lips. His shaggy eyebrows covered his still sharp green eyes; he opened his mouth to reveal teeth like the Devil's Causeway. He sighed, his eyes drowned in a grey soup of sorrow. Gwen's soft red hand gripped his drooping fingers trying to catch his eye.

*   *   *

Gwen, tall and slight, born in Poplar, was eight when she caught the train. Then she had her hair in rags to get her to look like an angel - which she wasn't. Catching the train was a blessed relief from school and the nightly bombing. Jack had come from West Ham; he was six. His parents had been anxious to get him away on Operation Pied Piper but he had been ill, so he now accompanied Daisy, same age, a stranger from Stepney. Boarding the train she sounded the happiest of them all, although after the train left she soon wet herself. Frightened and alone no one knew where they were going. Secured to each child was a big brown label with their name and home address, gas mask and one small suitcase with all their worldly possessions. Daisy had left home wearing a vest, pullover and dirndl skirt, cut below her knees, with white ankle socks. Jack wore long shorts, with regulation braces and a pullover. The colours were all dull except for those worn by Patricia. Pat from Bloomsbury, only four and a half, small, well spoken, quiet and feisty. Her parents had failed to get her on the boat for Canada despite her father's wealth and position as a Government scientist working on top secret projects. She had been taken to the railway station directly in her parent's car, not on the bus; she stood out in her blue beret, gymslip, white blouse and blue coat. Little did she realise that she would be the catalyst for an adventure.

They all bundled into the carriage; it was a newer one with a corridor and a lavatory at the end. No roll call; there was enough to do just getting them on board. Many of the little blighters fought to stay with their friends and families. Small, many under five, hopeless and thrust into a topsy turvey world; for some it was the first time on a train. Absorbed in their surroundings, they were quiet, white faced, tears streaming softly, shocked at leaving their home and loved ones; only the clanking and roll of the iron wheels could be heard. London, still smouldering, passed behind them in a blue haze, they gazed out wondering when they would see it again and be comforted by the fireside at home.

Lanky Gwen was the first to perk up.

'Daisy you need a change. Let me take you to the lav, bring your case and we will get you sorted. Jack, make sure no one comes in and bags our seats.'

Gwen eyed the little girl with blonde curly hair and innocent eyes, her lower lip trembling.

'What's your name ducky? You can come with us too. Let's stick together.' They slide open the carriage door and smell the smoke as little black smuts sweep in making their faces dirty. The girls quickly close the door. Jack ponders alone as he looks out at a new planet of green fields, cows and occasional horse. The sky is a misty blue which soon turns into a crimson bower as the sun sets beyond the August horizon. The train clatters along. An incandescent glow radiates from the ceiling; just enough to see the tired bodies, arms clasped around one another. They look like sleeping angels.

There is a movement. Jack opens an eye. Patricia untangles arms and legs and creeps towards the door. He helps her slide the door open; then closes it. He is soon back to sleep. The rhythm of the train's clickety clack, clickety clack, keeps the children in slumber. At one point the train stops as an air raid goes on over Oxford. Soon there is a jarring of wheels, the rushing of billowing steam and the dullest of lights as the train enters the station.

The children wake at once and press their noses to the window.

'No signs here,' says Jack.

'Somewhere north,' says Gwen, but neither knew where they were. Doors are opened; the big leather strap hangs there. It is used for opening the window. Someone opens the tap and the dirty, weary, hair- matted evacuees drip onto the platform.

'Where's the blonde kid?' says Daisy.

'Oh! She left to join the posh kids further up the corridor', replies Jack.

They are soon assembled and led to waiting buses. The adults go too but like the children are half asleep. Arriving at the village hall they are met by local folk who speak differently. The children huddle closer together. One by one, or sometimes in twos, they are peeled off, like skins off an onion. Suddenly only Jack, Gwen and Daisy are left.

'Albert, can we take all three? They'll be useful on the farm'.

'They're not very big. Are you sure you can cope, two girls and a boy? They're coming here for school so that's an easy walk from the farm. Keeping them together may be a good idea. Ain't got much poor beggars. Let's get home and give them a clean. A good bit of grub won't do them no harm either.' The small party were the last to leave, carrying what little they had to the Naylors' farm on the edge of the village. Fed and watered they were soon sound asleep in a big horsehair-filled mattress; the children would fill the barren dreams of the farmers and should have a peaceful life.

In the first few days they were quiet, submissive and burdened by change. The children soon realised in the quiet there were no bangs from the bombs, no smell of fright and nobody huddled in Anderson shelters for hours; there were no shelters in the village but they did pull the blinds down at night. Stars were plentiful and illuminating; sheep were left to wander the lanes and in the village shop a ration book was still demanded.

'We have a simple village,' said the shopkeeper 'It's not London, full of fish 'n chip shops, jellied eels and spivs.'

There was a knock on the farm door. Albert opens it to see a Police Inspector.

'Mabel get the kids to come down, Joe is here in his official capacity; he wants to question them. The bobbies must be worried to send Joe.'

Mabel bustled and rounded up her gang of three. She showed no concern; in her short acquaintance she found them polite, quiet and honest. The children arrived in a joyful mood. He saw three waifs; with a paternal sympathy he was gentle with his questioning.

'We have reason to believe that a young girl with blonde curly hair was in the same carriage as you when you left London but did not arrive in Northampton. Have you any idea what happened to her? Her name was Patricia.'

The children stood, rooted. Surely she had arrived at the station? They were all confused but Jack had felt his cheeks beginning to burn. He coughed, glanced down and wanted to pee. Moving from foot to foot he felt eyes lancing his body.

'Well Jack, it seems as if you know something'

'I only slid the door open when she wanted to go to the lav.

We were all asleep, it was dark and she could not push the door herself. I must 'ave fallen asleep again. When I woke I just thought she must have gone up the corridor to be with those posh kids so said nuffin'; seemed sensible to me. We never saw 'er again. We all thought she 'ad gone off with the lah-di-dah people who collected the gymslip group. They all went off in big cars'.

The Inspector looked at the two girls who were nodding their heads like Muffin the Mule. With eyes oozing tears and confused as to why this big uniformed man thought they should know something, they withdrew. The inspector quickly sensed that they were telling the truth. He thanked Mabel, told Albert he would not be troubling them again and left silently. The household sighed with relief. Their new guardians were left thinking of the little girl lost in the Northampton countryside. Gwen sucked her dangling plaits. As the eldest she worried that she should she have done more. The lav had been a long way down the corridor; she should have gone with her. Daisy remained reflective; she had taken little notice of the small cuddly child. Daisy thought she spoke too posh anyway, not from our end of town.

The episode was a closed book. No one mentioned the loss

and disappearance of Patricia. Perhaps they were all thinking that they could have done something different to change the way things happen but we all know life is set. The children were assigned duties. Gwen being tall and strong for her age was given milking lessons by Albert. She had to get up very early but was rewarded with gentle cows, kindness from Albert and lots of milk. She had a man she could look up to. He never hit her and hardly raised his voice, such a change. Her school work was basic. They all worked in the same big school room, only divided by wide aisles. The teacher taught them how to do sums, to read and to write. Gwen encouraged Jack and Daisy and heard them read every night. Sometimes Mabel would listen but she never helped them with their writing or sums. She relied on Gwen. Mabel was happy to teach her brood how to do basic cooking, even though the farm flour was in short supply; wet Saturdays were baking days, a treat.

The girls had visits from their mothers. Gwen was left traumatised after one visit as her mother hardly spoke. The bombing had been particularly bad in their part of London. She kept telling her daughter that she was best off with Mabel. Gwen was very sad when she waved her mum off. Stepney was badly damaged but

Daisy's mum was quite cheerful. She was obviously pleased to see her daughter, but wept in gratitude for the care Mabel and Albert had shown her daughter. Jack only had one visit, surprisingly, from his dad. He explained to Jack that his mother had to look after the shop.

'Jack you're a chip off the old block,' was all Albert said after Jack's father had left. Jack never saw his Dad again whilst at the farm.

The children often walked up the mile lane to the big house. The 'big house' was home for disabled boys. They were some of the lucky handicapped children to have been evacuated, many weren't. Despite their loss of limbs or inability to do what most kids could do they were happy and never put up any barriers. The 'big house' was supervised by a strange 'snooty' couple who, if they saw any of the evacuee 'gang', despised them and would tell them to 'be off back to your village.' The housekeeper and other maids were more sympathetic as they knew their charges enjoyed the company of the ragamuffins from the city. They 'spoke funny', had weird games which they taught the 'big house' kids, but most of all the cockneys never seemed to see the disabilities and shortcomings of their new mates. They spent many an hour playing together and learning things such as how to fish or make a trolley so some of them could be carried further afield. They all liked to sneak off to the fields where the Italian prisoners of war worked. The Italians loved to speak to the children in their broken English which improved over time, even though they found some of the cockney dialect hard to understand. The evacuees loved the Italians and in return the Italians gave them unbridled love. No Italian ever escaped.

The Police called in again but it was to tell Gwen that her mother and father had been killed in a bombing raid. Their house had just collapsed. Shortly after that they came again to pass on a similar dispatch to Daisy. The two girls were distraught, but with the love and kindness from their adoptive parents, they kept going. When the Police came again fear flamed the family. Mabel grasped Jack to her side; surely Jack could not lose his parents too.

This time they had come to make more enquiries about the little girl Patricia. Alas no more could be said and the Police left with just a plea that if the children heard anything they must pass it on. They did reveal there was no mistake; she had not been taken accidentally to any other house.

'If you hear anything don't bottle it up, tell you Aunty or Uncle Bert. They will let us know. You know we have resources and we may just need your piece of jigsaw to complete the picture. We have good reason to believe Pat is still alive. She may have been taken off the train by someone who has hidden her. We know you kids have good eyes and ears so sniff it out. You can be our extended arms and who knows there may be a reward.'

'Ooh! Did you 'ear that Jack? A reward? 'ow much? We will have elephant ears and doggie noses; we will help you find that girl!' Gwen beamed a confident grin at the detective as he left to go. They had no idea where to start to look for the blonde haired Shirley Temple lookalike. Overnight they became bloodhounds.

Farm life progressed happily but the thought of the reward was always in their heads. It was Jack that first picked up the vibes. The 'snooties' were more anxious than ever that the evacuees should not enter the 'big house', which was like honey for the bee. He heard one of the amputees saying to his younger partially blind friend that he had heard a young girl crying in the night but she never came down to breakfast. Jack had never seen a little girl at the place. He was curious. He gently asked more of the 'big house' kids if they had seen or heard of a little girl. Like the policeman said, little bits of a jigsaw can make a picture and so it was; Jack was convinced a little girl was hidden in the 'big house'. How could he enter the place to search it?

As time progressed their sleep was often interrupted by the continuous overflying of German bombers on their way to bomb Coventry and other industrial centres in the Midlands. On return flights back to Nazi Germany the bombers regularly released unused bombs into local fields; fortunately none fell onto the village. Daisy had many a sleepless night worrying that the bombers could see their blazing hearth by looking straight down their chimney. Albert had to call in the Army bomb squad one day as a stick of bombs fell on the large field reserved for the cows. None of the bombs had exploded. It was a long job for the Army making all the bombs safe. The field was the main centre of attention for all the children, trying to collect souvenirs until Albert told Jack to stop his mates from invading the area. They drifted back to seeing the children in the 'big house'.

The bang, vibration, kitchen crockery crashing and smashing windows rocked them from their beds. Albert shouted for everyone to assemble downstairs. There were no fires in the village but all the windows were broken. It was not a normal bomb but a gigantic bomb which could not have dropped from a plane but where had it come from? It was only as the sun rose that the complete devastation was revealed. The Army arrived early in a big truck and were soon encouraging the children to look for shrapnel. Jack and his two adopted sisters had other ideas and were soon off to the 'big house' to check on their other friends. The lady of the house had been badly cut by flying glass and had been taken to hospital by her husband. This was Jack's chance. He slid into the house whilst Gwen and Daisy kept the housekeeper in conversation about the explosion. Straight up the stairs, he searched, occasionally calling 'Patricia', convinced she was there somewhere.

He had just reached the attic when he heard the whimpering. He rushed to the door which was locked. He searched the area, using a stool he was able to run his hand over the top frame of the door. The key dropped to the floor. Quickly he unlocked the door and ran in. The wind was blowing through the broken window. Patricia was curled up in the darkened corner. She had grown but he knew her immediately. He quickly told her to get dressed. She recognised Jack and held his hand tightly. Running down the stairs Jack helped the young girl down the big stone steps onto the grass. He took her into the woods that led them to the farm.

'Well, well, who have we here, Jack?' Mabel's eyes were wide and reflective.

'This is Patricia, the little girl who was lost on our train.' Jack explained that he had found her in the 'big house'. 'Gwen and Daisy are still up there but they should be back shortly.'

Suddenly there was a knocking on the kitchen door. Mabel scooped Pat into her arms and bundled her onto the big bed. Indicating to Pat to keep quiet she went downstairs to answer the door. It was the Army.

'Have your kids managed to pick up any shrapnel Mrs. Naylor? Sorry to trouble you but we have strict orders to collect it all in. I believe the boffins are baffled as they've never seen a flying bomb, a 'Doodlebug', this far north before. I haven't told you that, you know walls have ears. All the sheep penned in the centre of the village have been killed and no house has been left undamaged. It was a big bomb.'

Mabel nearly crumpled but was able to reassure the soldier that the children were all doing their jobs on the farm and had no time for rummaging. The soldier left whistling. As soon as he had gone she rushed upstairs and soon had Pat undressed and put into the big tin bath in the kitchen. She was scrubbed and smelt like a rose. Mabel had secreted a bar for a special occasion. Kids smelt and Pat smelt like ripe cheese before her bath. Pat was dressed in Daisy's old clothes, which had been washed and saved. What was she to tell Albert?

'There's only one thing to do. The kids have done a great job but we have to have that child down to Joe as soon as we can. Obviously there has been a crime so we should keep it quiet. Tell the children to stay in and we'll take the girl to the Police Station.'

Mabel and Albert tucked Pat between them in their small truck and left to find Joe. The children said their goodbyes and a relieved Jack even managed a hug. That was the last they saw of Pat on that sombre afternoon towards the end of the war.

*   *   *

Looking around Phyllis realised that there was still an icy gap between Jack and the two women. Jack was sullen and had not said much. The women admitted they had remained at the farm and had eventually been adopted by Mabel and Albert. Daisy had married at eighteen and Gwen much later to a widowed farmer. They were both widows now. Phyllis eventually prised some information from Jack.

'Just remind me where you met? Was it planned in the war?'

'No, we met on a train, just kids clinging together as they did going to Auschwitz. I loved that farm. I went back to my dad. My mum had gone so we had a hard time in bombed out London. When I could I joined the Army and life was better. I often thought of Pat and rescuing her.' He blushed with pride. Phyllis bit her tongue, her surprise was about to be exposed. She checked her watch.

The pub door opened and a freezing blast caught their feet. In walked a tanned attractive blonde lady who made her way to the bar. Phyllis was up taking her by the hand.

'Hello, I believe you are Pat, welcome back. I am Phyllis Abercrombie who invited you here. I am so happy you were able to make it,' she spoke rapidly, 'I am sure you are longing to meet Gwen, Daisy and Jack.'

Tears brimmed in Pat's sparkling eyes. When she spoke it was with a Tennessee drawl. A face, lined from too much exposure to the sun, smiled. A slim figure, brightly dressed she looked outstanding.

'Hi! I am so glad to be here. I've just flown in to Heathrow and can't wait to meet them.'

Suddenly Gwen, crying tears of happiness, hugged Pat followed hesitantly by Daisy. Jack reticent, uncurled and shook her hand, his eyes never leaving her face. This was the little girl he had rescued those many years ago. Was she really as old as he was? They sat, the girls talking non-stop with the occasional word from Jack. Pat held all their hands in a bunch.

'Well folks it has been wonderful to meet you and I do thank Phyllis for arranging this. I owe you an explanation. In the beginning I should have gone to Canada on the 'City of Bandares' that sunk with a loss of many children. When I caught the train with you I was kidnapped. My Dad was shocked when he received a ransom note from those people who owned the 'big house'. Thanks to you he never had to pay it but after I arrived home we suddenly left for the USA. The owners of the 'big house' were caught and jailed; to this day I don't know if they wanted secrets or cash. I finished up in Sewanee, Tennessee. Sadly my parents have passed on but they always wanted you to receive a reward. I have now fulfilled their wishes by bringing each of you a cheque for £150,000.' Their eyes glazed over, but Jack was able to stammer,

'Oh! Crikey Pat, thank you, but saving you was the best thing I ever did in the war!'

The other two, sobbing, clasped their benefactor. A bond forged in desperate times was rekindled never ever to be broken.

A Village By-Pass

The man picked up the red singing and dancing phone. The black, broad brimmed hat hid his face and he drawled into the mouthpiece. His shoulders drooped as the conversation continued; he prodded the ground with his sharp pointed toe. It pawed the ground like a horse in a dressage competition. He was large, one could see his chest expanding and then there was stasis, silence, the wind died. He lowered the phone and walked absently down the tree lined village street. His trouser turn-ups collected the falling rain drops; he wiped his suntanned face and swung open the pub door. The drinking men stepped aside as the barge of a man made his way to the bar. The publican not used to seeing the large man in such an elegiac mood eyed him closely. The man turned his back to the bar and undid his soaking cloak. He was smart with a shirt, tie and a Saville Row suit. He made his way to the snug.

The pub was small, enough to cater for the village folk but not for the visitors. That day it was bursting, being a Tuesday and a farmer's market. The smell of pigs and cows pervaded the air; dragged into the bar on the shoes and clothes of the farmers. The publican, Mr Dick Henry was an affable chap who always welcomed his customers with a hale and hearty greeting which was nearly always reciprocated except for the likes of Mr. Fox and his club. They thought they owned the village and all should bow and scrape, they had not realised times had moved on.

It was the new generation that was wielding the power; children bred to the middle and lower classes whose parents lived in the small cottages. David Mellor, the village cabinet maker was such a person. His son had become a designer of fine furniture and sold to all the 'big' houses. David was a great lover of country values and was vocal when changes were raised by the village or parish council. However the one decision he was willing to put his weight behind was the village by-pass. Having the by-pass would help save the village and its traditions. It was visionary.

Mr. Fox, on the other hand was not so sure. Traffic by-passing the village would lose valuable customers and the cattle market might even get moved. He was noticed making his way through the bar looking like a bull; he was often like this so people just moved aside.

The clock chimed eleven which reminded Kevin that the decision should have been made. The rain wasn't helping with his mood. He had little hope that it would go in his favour. The rich and beautiful of the village had too much clout. He rolled his big eyes, pulled his short coat around his shoulders and slowly walked down the wet reflecting cobbled pavement. He needed to get to the pub. He had worked hard with the committee to get the resolution passed. He was white faced and worn. He was wise in wit and steeped in the history of the village. He loved his ancient village and his many loyal friends that lived in the brick and stone clad houses. He had spent the night talking and going over the arguments his friends had placed before the County enquiry. He loved Geraldine for her enthusiasm, was grateful for the pen of Phyllis and her well written pleas and so grateful to Donald for his never ending loyal support. Dressed in his roll neck pullover, corduroy trousers and wellington boots he looked every inch a country yokel. His mind was sharp, magical words rolled off his tongue. Perhaps he was wrong, they would succeed.

It had been a long and arduous task persuading the village that the by-pass would be a good thing for the community but Mr Mellors had formed a very able committee to face the force of Mr Fox and his business colleagues. They were adamant that the cost of the by-pass was unjustified. Plus the possibility of moving the cattle market and building the new estate, not as was presently planned at the end of the village, but moved to the end of the dual carriageway closer to Kilworth, three miles away. To them it was a waste of money and a great financial loss to the community. Who was going to win the County Planning decision? There was a lot at stake but it was gradually dawning on those who had little capital to make, that Mellors and his gang may be right and the village in all its glory could remain the same. Some of the County Council came to see the village and have a meal in the pub. They experienced the atmosphere and despite being hosted by the Fox Group had enough vocal intervention, by other locals, to realise it was a difficult decision to pass. Time dragged on and Tuesday, today was the day of the announcement.

The women of the village had a big say. They wanted the by-pass for the children's sake; no more fast cars and big lorries rushing by the school. The fish and chip shop was definitely on the Fox side. A lot of their trade was from 'passing folk'. The farmers were split; some said a new market and new facilities would be welcomed.

Fox caught Mellor's eye, they filled with light and grew big, very big. Was Fox going to collapse or turn into a monster?

'Ah! Mellor the by-pass decision has been made. They start building in six months. You and your committee may be well pleased.'

Mr. Kevin Mellor felt the warmth of victory spread from his neck, through his lungs, his legs to his small weaselled toes,

'Thank you Mr Fox. That will be most welcomed'.

'Ah! But the new housing estate is going to be built in the field next to the Post Office so we shall still have summat'.

The Neighbour

James strolled through the high hedged path; he was going to post a letter that should have gone days ago. It was a lovely spring morning, fresh clean air and blue skies, his nerves relaxed.

She smiled, as only a young bright eyed young girl could, as she put the letter in the 'to go' bag. The Post Office in Great Glen is one that you would imagine benefits a rural village. Old but new, clean and organised with the stuff you might need yet carrying all the essentials. Sue was the manageress, efficient and friendly, with the silent, but always present, grey haired figure of her husband Graham. He could have been the icon who was forever Postman Pat's right hand man. Behind the counter were those bright young ladies, chosen above all for their smiles. You could have said that you had an elephant to post. They would say with that warm glow, 'Please put it on the scales', and then plaster it with stamps. Nothing was too much for them.

James strolled back home, the village was being overrun by cars, creating noise, parking problems and pollution. All the streets had been named after the places and people that had participated in the nearby battle of Naseby in 1576. Prince Rupert had escaped to a house on Main Street; his troops had slept in the church. Take a stroll in the depths of night and see their ghosts. Not much happened in Glen until August when there was the annual wheelbarrow race which was feted and talked about 'til the following August.

James' gait was slow; it was a steep hill up to Edgehill. Christine always puffed which wasn't surprising as she was a London evacuee. She worked in Park Lane when she was fifteen and remained at her post when the bombs fell. Were hotel workers given 'war medals'?

Turning the corner James first saw him in his garage, bending over. The new neighbour was laying a wooden floor. He was a man of about eighty. He was about five foot six, balancing his glasses on his thin nose, slight but fit.

'Good afternoon', it was softly spoken with a foreign balm, was he French? He worked quietly and skilfully slotting the wooden panels into one another. The garage floor was becoming a completed jigsaw.

'That looks good', James said, 'You must be new around here, are you a carpenter, joiner or just a handyman?'

He looked up, smiled, and said 'I needed to have the floor covered so I have done it myself. I have just moved in'. I was curious; he was either a very good English speaker or had acquired his French lilt from years of living with the natives.

'Where are you from?' James felt rude asking another question but he had to establish the link of his accent. 'Oh! My wife Ruth and I have just come from Brazzaville, do you know it?'

James' legs flexed, 'Yes, I do, I lived in Kinshasa some time ago'.

There they were on a cold winter's day, hands frozen, both of them thinking of hot steamier times. No wonder he had a French accent if he had been living out there for years. James knew French was the main language used by the Congolese government. If you wanted to communicate with the leaders and the various tribes around the Congo one had to speak French or Belgian French; was he a Walloon? James, a retired mercenary, had come to hide in this small Leicestershire estate. Was there now a neighbour with a past to hide? Perhaps his new neighbour had also been driven out and fled to this peaceful place.

James pondered awhile, should he pursue the matter, what could this chap have done in far off Africa? The challenge was to find out but the new neighbour was not to enquire about James' murky past. He may have even heard of him, as Brazzaville was just across the river from Kinshasa. James had spent years supporting black men and their Governments. The intrigue and the covering up of a life he would not admit to, it had worn him down. He had fought off diseases, the evil things that he had had to do and had left the country in an emaciated state; all he wanted was a quiet life. Was he now facing an old enemy, spy or a skilled retired mercenary like himself?

James thought of another tack, relax. Forget Africa and concentrate on the present and look to the future. His mind could not think straight so many ghastly images had reared up in his mind. He could feel his wet clammy hands releasing the magazine he had in his hand. He had to think rapidly, 'Could you help me with my garage floor?'

The neighbour turned, grinned, 'I would be delighted. I did this when we were refurbishing our Salvation Army hostels in Africa; there wooden floors rotted so quickly.' James was relieved;

he had only found a Sally Ann volunteer. He wondered if he was a simple chap who would know little of the outside world. Was he beyond giving tea and buns and refurbishing hostels? He introduced himself and told the sprightly old man that he was a neighbour a few doors down. He instantly like this chap but his mind could not accept this elderly craftsman as naive; he was gently intrigued.

'My name is Bramwell Booth. My wife Ruth and I have just moved to Great Glen. We belong to the Salvation Army; perhaps you have heard of my Grandfather?'

James blanked his emotions; he was humbled. Here was a couple that certainly knew about the world and its problems. He was to learn, later, about the neighbour's French mother, the escape from France at the beginning of WW II and the many adventures they had in a multitude of countries working for the Sally Ann. What a revelation!

He drifted down the Close to his home. The warmth and security that filled him reassured him that he and Bramwell would soon become good neighbours. His secrets were safe.

The cockpit of the Constellation in the Maltese Air Museum

The Constellation on the Luqa Apron, Malta

The Maltese Constellation

A search of the internet will reveal some photographs and a brief history about an aircraft that arrived in Malta one night in the 1960s.

The aircraft, a Lockheed Super Constellation, appeared in mysterious circumstances on the quick reaction apron (QRA), which was just off the main runway. The QRA was used by RAF fighters when they were based there at the time of the Cold War. The Constellation was a queen of the skies. In its day it produced a similar public reaction to the one that greeted the supersonic Concorde; it was a head turner with beautiful lines. The distinct sound of the Constellation's four piston engines in a sleek and fast aeroplane was a pointer in the development of post war aviation. Inside the aircraft the passengers were treated to large comfortable seats. The lucky ones could sit round a table fitted between facing seats and observe the world passing by through large clear windows. It never flew that high, unlike the modern airliner; one looked forward to flying in the 'Connie'.

This particular aircraft was delivered to the Portuguese airline, TAP, in 1955. It was operated by them for many years until 1967 when it was bought by the North American Aircraft Company and used, under a false registration, in the horrendous war in Biafra, a scourge in the history of Africa. It was then mysteriously flown and abandoned in Malta. After years of loneliness the abandoned aircraft was acquired by the Government. No owner was forthcoming and the parking fees had become greater than the value of the aircraft.

The Government sold it for £M3000. In 1973 she was towed to the nearby village of Kirkop and made into a restaurant with most of the cockpit and instrumentation left intact. Fourteen years later it was closed down and lay silent until the Maltese Aviation Museum showed interest in restoring the old lady. Sadly it was not to be and vandals attacked it first, destroying it by fire on the 30th January in 1997.

This is a story of what may have happened when the aircraft 'mysteriously' arrived that night in 1968 in Malta and was abandoned by the crew. It is up to you, the reader, to decide if this could have happened. Read on...

The Constellation Story

Last week an article in the Daily Telegraph stirred some memories, it was reported that a Lockheed Constellation aircraft had been removed from the runway apron at Luqa, Malta. It had been there for some time, an eyesore and an enigma. No one had claimed it. It had just become the property of the Maltese Government as the parking fees had exceeded the value of the aircraft.

Many years ago I was a junior officer working at Luton airport when I first saw that aircraft, about to take off, very shiny with green lettering. All I knew was that it was owned by an American company. It was soon airborne and turned South. Where to I never found out?

'We have a charter', the Commercial Manager addressed his Senior Captain, 'Martin, I think you will have to take it. It's a quick job, just flying some BP workers to Libya'.

Martin rubbed his long shrapnel scar with his sausage like fingers; the scar ran down his left cheek. Captain Martin Blain smiled. He was a stocky man with a dark head of hair punctuated with tufts of grey. He never spoke much and when he did you could hear a Birmingham burr. He was educated at George Dixon's Grammar in Edgbaston, then up to Birmingham University until the war intervened. He had joined the RAF and stayed until the end of the Berlin airlift in 1949. Martin always had shiny shoes, get close enough and you could smell the Kiwi polish.

'You will have fifty passengers to fly from Heathrow to El Adem. An easy trip, a night stop then back empty the following day. Will you take the usual crew?'

Martin ruminated, his crew were his co-pilot, Edward 'Ted' Beech, flight engineer Billy Potts and two stewardesses Jenny Dixon and Jacqueline Hill; they all worked well together.

Ted had been fortunate; his father had paid for his flight training. Initially on an old bi-plane, a Tiger Moth, then he had graduated to the twin engine Airspeed Oxford. The tall, slim, green eyed young man had had a chance meeting with Captain Blain in the Savoy Grille, which resulted in an offer to fly the four engine beauty. It took several weeks of hard training before the Captain was satisfied that his co-pilot would be able to land the aircraft, should he collapse.

The Lockheed Constellation, affectionately known as 'the Connie', was developed after WWII as a commercial airliner. It had four super charged engines, each one powering a three bladed propeller, seating eighty people in armchair comfort and equipped with large panoramic windows. This was a bonus as their aircraft flew unpressurised below ten thousand feet giving passengers a wonderful view of the world below.

The passenger terminal at Heathrow had just been changed from a tented enclosure, large marquees, to one with the latest prefabricated buildings. The BP passengers checked in and were loaded. Soon the engines were started in sequence, starting with the number four, the outer engine on the starboard side. Once all the engines were growling, Jenny picked up her microphone to begin the briefing. She was just over the minimum height of five foot four, sharp beady eyes, short brown hair with petite hands and feet. She was Scottish and was rumoured to be heiress to a large country estate so she felt she had no need for a husband.

Jacqueline Hill, known to her friends as Jackie, lived in Hendon, where the Flight Centre is based. She was a receptionist there until she met Martin Blain who persuaded her that she should see the world and join his outfit. She was a farmer's daughter from the Shires, charming, well spoken, with a beautiful oval face. She loved wearing fine clothes and her diamond cluster broach, small but significant, always produced comment when she wore it to work. Jackie was never short of a party invitation so it was exciting to use as an excuse that she was off to Africa.

After the passenger briefing the aircraft, unique with its three rudders, soared aloft heading for Paris, Lyon and beyond. It was a smooth and uneventful ride.

'What's wrong with this lot?' said a frustrated Jackie, 'None of them want a drop of liquor, have BP stopped paying them or are they just tight?'

'It's a mystery to me too. They all look strong and well worn but they all sit there looking comatose. Oil exploration in Libya must be a demanding challenge.'

The engines droned on, they changed pitch at one point as they climbed over the Alps, passing Mont Blanc, down the Aosta valley and across the Po River to Milan. They were soon over Genoa flying South. They crossed the Mediterranean from Sicily towards the North African coast.

Soon the power and noise reduced as they flew a cruise descent down to El Adem. By now the setting sun was blazing, reflecting bright golden hues off the sandy beaches. The cabin became sticky but the girls looked fresh in their crisp white blouses as they checked the seats for landing.

A smooth touch-down was followed by a slow taxi to the apron. The steps were brought to the aircraft and eighty weary passengers, carrying a lot of hand luggage, disembarked. Jenny and Jackie did a final sweep of the cabin. They found a clip of .303 ammunition. Jenny took it to the Captain. He was folding up the charts; Bill was filling in the technical log whilst Ted was trying to order some fuel. One never knew when they might get a sudden charter.

'I found this Captain, should I leave it here or take it to the Customs?'

'Let's have no trouble. Just leave it in a seat pocket and we will sort it out in Luton.'

They were booked into the Marhaba hotel, not five star but good enough for weary aircrew. The sun was setting and from the souk, the market, the odour of a day's trading. The short fearful taxi ride was worth a hundred flying hours of stress, an ice cold beer was becoming more appealing by the minute. After checking in they were soon showered, changed and sipping their first drink. It was the usual, beer for the boys and Martinis for the girls.

After a couple of welcome drinks they retired to the restaurant. The evening's menu was lamb with couscous or rice, if preferred. There was little flirting. Bill was happy to retire early and no one made a move to get closer. At ten the stewardesses made their excuses and left. Jenny was pleased that she was sharing with Jackie as the atmosphere was making her a little insecure. Ted and Bill were in the same room on the second floor. Martin climbed the stairs to his suite, quite suitable for a Captain.

They were blasted awake by a loud explosion and violent noises from below. Doors crashed open. Martin was up, dressed and rushing down the corridor towards the girls' room, he was intercepted by Ted and Bill who had the same paternal idea. Martin banged on the door which was opened by a pale faced Jackie.

'Are you OK? Something is obviously going on so I suggest we stay tight together until things quieten down'. This was not a suggestion but an order from the Captain. Doors were slammed and broken, the sounds came closer. Their door was hit and an Arabic command was given. Martin opened the door.

'Out! Out! Go downstairs we need you!' An Arab soldier in a rag bag uniform was making it perfectly clear that they had no choice.

They were hustled downstairs. Once in the foyer Martin was thrust forcibly into a side room. Men in dark uniforms followed him in. Ted and Bill stood protectively around Jenny and Jackie. No one spoke a word as they were all well aware of the predicament they were in. Another large vehicle screamed to a halt outside the hotel and from it descended a well dressed, tall Arab who left a trail of pungent aroma of Arabic perfume. He entered the room that held Martin; there was no doubt that they knew that he was their Captain. The remaining crew hoped and prayed he would not be beaten, who else would fly them home?

It was a long hour before the remaining crew were told to return to their rooms. They selected to gather in Ted and Bill's room as it was further down the corridor.

Guns could be heard, excited Arabs were firing blindly into the night sky, sounds of mortars thudding into the other side of town and flares lighting up the black, brown city. Suddenly peace, an enforced silence, someone had turned a knob and the city sat in darkness.

Just what had the crew flown into? Martin appeared within minutes, worn but unharmed without any apparent signs of him having been tortured.

'It would appear that we have flown into a revolution. They say that King Idris has been deposed by a Colonel Ghaddafi, who has taken over. Our passengers were not BP employees and I think we could be here for awhile. Best if we made ourselves comfortable'.

Jenny had brought some supplies from the aircraft's bar. It was silly to be taking all that alcohol back to Luton, but their drinking would be limited because of the situation they were in. They decided that they would all stay in the same room; as the Captain's suite was the largest they moved in there. Jackie began to weep but before Ted could move Jenny had her arms around her. She looked like a doting mother. Martin admitted that he thought the passengers were military personnel, particularly as they had found the clip of ammunition. They slept, the girls in the large bed whilst the boys slept on the sofas and arm chair.

They were cooped up in that hotel for days with no outside contact. Eventually Martin was able to persuade the security officer that there was an oil leak on the aircraft and that it needed repairing. Late in the afternoon a truck arrived to take him and Bill to the aeroplane. Martin then persuaded the security people that the whole crew needed to go to the aircraft for various reasons. The guard was quite amicable after a donation of a few whiskies. They all piled into the vehicle. Martin had told them to carry anything they could hide in their uniforms, but most importantly they would need their passports, which had been returned by reception.

A crumpled crew left the hotel after five days with no outside contact. However the Captain and Engineer had made a plan. In Bill's flight bag were the runway performance charts with which Martin was able to calculate the distance needed for a take-off. The aircraft was parked at the far end of the apron so their plan had a chance of success. The truck dropped them at the bottom of the aircraft steps. Bill took time and effort in unscrewing the engine panels, inspecting them and then securing them back. He then persuaded the ground crew to remove the steps, explaining that they may blow backwards into the tail, once the engines were giving power.

The two stewardesses secured the cabin, by now they had been told about the escape plan. Frightened but confident in the Captain's skill to fly them away they secured themselves to the forward bulkhead. It was important now not to arouse suspicion. At five o'clock most of the airport staff would be going home, at six the airport closed. The field was surrounded by tanks and light armoured vehicles, but the orb of the setting sun would aid their escape.

The two inner engines were started, belching black smoke, happy to be alive. They would give the aircraft hydraulic power for the flaps, vital for a short take off run, nose wheel steering and eventually power to raise the undercarriage. The Captain wanted to start the other two engines at the same time. This required very good crew co-operation. They all realised that once started they would have little time to warm them up before demanding take-off power. Fortunately it had been a hot day and the engine oil was already warm. The props turned, creating bigger clouds of belching black smoke, soon all the engines were running.

Brakes were released and the big aeroplane began to roll across the empty apron, gathering speed it swung onto the taxiway and soon it had enough speed to take off. The attitude of the aircraft did not change but the wheels came up; the aircraft remained level so they were flying very low. Pointed directly into the setting sun it was difficult for the Arab gunners to see the aircraft; it flew over the sand and settled to flying at a height of fifty feet over the ocean and away to Malta.

The rest is history. The Constellation arrived in Malta unannounced, landing in the silent night without the use of any lights. It parked just at the end of the runway in the large apron. It was not many minutes before the crew had abandoned the aircraft and disappeared.

I met up with Captain Blain years later. When I spoke about the Constellation he kept tight lipped. I am sure he had been aware that they were carrying troops to aid King Idris. Sadly the troops arrived too late and had evaporated into the Sahara but Her Majesty's Government would never admit to that. I suspect Martin Blain had selected that crew for just such a job. The pilots flew again, Bill went on to teach engineering and Jenny became lady of the Manor. I read that Ted Beech married Jacqueline Hill a few years ago, I was pleased about that. I wondered if they were ever told the truth, I wonder?

The Friday that Changed the face of the Middle East

The sun shone fiercely; a big pale blue sky filled the canvas. The lazy buzzard circled round and round looking for prey. Life was still; until the Land Rover drew up and stopped. This was Jordan, a new name for the desert kingdom; it had been Trans Jordan, ruled by King Abdulla 1, an Emir who had an accountable history. Silence. The people in the truck waited, wet with sweat, They were overlooking the airfield in Amman where a red carpet had been laid, soldiers were lined up on either side, rifles ready to salute the inbound King.

The young boy sat with his parents and sister. They had all been shopping at the NAAFI, the grocery store that was in the RAF station in Amman. It was Friday, the Muslim day of rest. They had stopped to see the arrival of the King's aeroplane: he had been to Jerusalem to give an eulogy in the Mosque of Omar. The boy's father, an officer in the Arab Legion, had told his driver to stop. The boy waited in breathless anticipation to see the King alight from his plane.

Jordan, a jewel in the Middle East, had been at war with

Israel until 1948. With the diplomacy of the King and the British Government they had established a peace with the Jews. Thousands of Palestinians had to leave their homes and invaded the hinterland of Jordan. They set up large refugee camps, mainly around the large cities of Amman and Zerka.

Hot air rose, shimmering, creating mirages in the far desert.

The boy had dark hair, large green eyes and an insatiable curiosity. He looked placid as he peered down onto the scene. He searched for the small plane; aviation was exciting at his young age. He had often been taken away from school to be with his father; to explore the desert for Roman antiquities. Well that's what he saw. He was never told what other reasons there were for following the Hejaz railway or visiting the pumping stations in the Syrian Desert. It was just exciting to be off school for the day. It was a long way from home to the school in Amman. He liked school but he was more interested in the country and its people. He was not very tall, had various birth scars on his neck and a gash in his head, but he was bright and knew when to keep his mouth shut. His parents were vocal, were very popular and joined in all manner of activities, tennis, dancing and amateur dramatics. His mother often took him to the theatre to see his father perform on stage. They had a comfortable life. As for his sister, she spent most of her baby life with the nanny. Friday was her day off so the little girl sat quietly with her mother. All eyes were focused on the red carpet. The boy knew that his mother had been a favourite of the King. He has heard this from one of his parent's regular shouting matches. He hated those times and hid in his room when they started. He knew that his mother was very beautiful with her big eyes and wavy jet black hair. He loved her but even he was jealous at times; there was no nanny to love him. He did have a couple of friends who lived in the crescent who seemed to have similar parents.

'Children were to be seen but not heard', so it was good to be in a gang, his gang. His parents never knew about the stone throwing fights the gang had with the local Arab boys, they only heard about the pre-arranged school football games.

The boy looked on and noticed the soldiers were turning their rifles upside down, not one by one but haphazardly, awkwardly. He watched as if it was in slow motion, staring, but said nothing.

'Muhammad, take us home now', barked his father. They were all taken by surprise including Muhammad who had drifted into a world of his own. Starting the truck, crashing the gears they leapt forward. The boy looked at his mother. The colour had drained from her face as she clasped her little girl very tightly. His mother had been in the Army, and before that she had been a nurse and knew how to cope in a crisis. The boy became very disturbed as his mother looked very worried. There were no mobile phones, then, so what signal had spurred his father into such action? He smelt the sweat.

'Don't worry children your father has just remembered he has an appointment and we need to get home', she said unconvincingly. They all held on as the driver, not wishing to disobey his 'Effendi', drove rapidly towards home. Swirling sand was left trailing, obliterating the road behind.

Arriving at home the mother took the children to the boy's bedroom. It was large, full of toys with a four bladed fan turning day and night. There was no air conditioning and keeping the windows wide open at night gave some relief in the summer. Covered in mesh to keep out the flies it did not keep out the sound of the Mullah who cried for his faithful people to come to prayer, always as the sun rose at dawn. There was never a need for an alarm clock in their house. The children were put together and told to gather up some of their toys.

'We may all go on a picnic later', said their mother softly. The boy knew this was not a threat but a possibility. He helped his sister gather not only her toys but also some clothes she might need on a journey. His sister, young as she was, seemed to understand. She said nothing but opened drawers and cupboards to get her stuff. Too much but it was a good game. The boy had a better more compact pile of clothes which he pushed into his big school bag. He was empty of thought except that it was a lie, another one, which he was expected to comply with.

In the other part of the house raised voices could be heard, frightened and sometimes violent. There seemed to be great confusion. This was not the way a picnic adventure started. Thoughts swirled round his head. Were his parents about to abandon them as the Palestinian children had been? Arab children were poor. They were often left starving, dirty and ragged. He was happy in his life, his sister was happy, school was fun and he enjoyed learning, what was going to happen to all this? He cuddled his sister; a tear left the corner of his eye, smoothed down his cheek and dropped onto her golden hair. He shuddered. Where was their nanny? They both needed her loving arms even though she always murmured in softly slumberous Arabic. He was hungry and all the food had been left in the truck. Even he knew the butter would melt unless it was put in the ice box. Perhaps the cook had brought it in. What would happen to cook, gardener, and cleaning boys? Except for the noise from his parents it was quiet, the town was quiet and even the sky was still bright, blue and peaceful. He sighed and checked his sister. She had obviously had enough and had pulled the flower printed bed sheet over herself and gone to sleep. Long eyelashes, chubby face and short cuddly arms lay either side of her head. What a way to retreat when you are so innocent. He finished packing her bag squeezing the large pot doll with swivelling eyes, into every corner of the large satchel. They were ready to move. He felt pleased with himself but wanted to go to the lavatory. He crossed the passageway. The house was silent. Had everyone else left? No time to worry he had to have a pee.

He closed the lid of the 'thunder box' and washed his hands. He jumped and bit his tongue, there was banging on the front door. He heard the muffled voice of his father. It became louder, shouting, and then it became normal as he called for his wife. Mother appeared.

'Children we are not going on our picnic now but the cook will prepare us some lunch. Would you like some melon? We are going to have a treat of lamb and rice, would you please go into the garden and get some vine leaves for the cook '. His sister had woken up with the noise of the hammering on the door, she was whimpering softly.

They were not going to go anywhere: the boy was left to wander. His father must have received another message; perhaps his appointment had been canceled. It was sad that they had missed seeing the King, would he ever see King Abdulla?

He would never see King Abdulla; he had been assassinated at the Mosque of Omar by a Palestinian. The soldiers at the airfield had been turning their rifles, as per their Army regulations, in respect for their murdered King.

A stabilised country was now a dream, it was sliding downhill, a pattern that was set after WW I in the Hall of Mirrors in Versailles, had returned. There was no trust amongst the players of the world; it was going to be a bleak future for their children and grand children.

The Flash

The black and heavy clouds crossed the ridge

Outlined the Highlands sharp and chunky crags

His soaking skin and poor wretched dog

Plodded on through heather clad bogs

Deep recall, parched beaches and swaying palms

A brand new wife, shining eyes, deep in his arms

In Bali's sun, seas so deep, both wild and free

A forever life, that promised, ecstasy

Was it just ten years since the flash and crash

The black night, blood, horrendous gash

His eyes were gone, she so young, felt no pain

Held in time, what was the gain?

Slow the gait as they crossed the glen

A life imprisoned, in mind, maybe

Images, memories? No! He was free

Alas, 'to have and to hold'. Never again

This poem was written after the Bali bombing when several couples were killed

A Lost Love

Encased in memories, I lie alone

Where is she now, where has she gone?

To a far off land where I had planned

A togetherness

Oh! Sweet delights and Turkish nights

A desert still. Ah! Well she might

Have come to me, sweet asymmetry

But kismet cracks a pithy path

To hearts all bound with chains and locks

To drops of tears and diamond rocks

The chainmail curtain surrounds the throne

I am still here, I lie alone

Penarth Pier

Penarth Pier

The day was bright with shining sea

When I came at last to see, the pier

which was so old and strong, a giant

well rooted in deep dark black sand far below

the wide and flatness of the Bristol Channel, the distant shore,

Penarth Pier, eggshell blue, a veil of smoky green,

recovering now, of fishermen fishing, the pier was for all,

shadows lingering, the brass plaques, its ancient past,

ribboned along the lengths of trodden lathes, reminders of trysts,

friends and folks passed on, and current meetings,

we absorb the beauty that is Wales.

Silent Tears, Poems and other Stories

The Choice

Brrr. Brrr, Brrr. The phone rang. His fat fingers wrapped round the cradle and clamped the phone to his ear.

'Yes ... I have the latest weather. Yes the mist will fall in an hour. Where? In the Killiecrankie pass on the A9 ... Three climbers ... Avalanche.... Police and Mountain Rescue have been advised. ...We will call you with an estimated overhead time.' One hand put the phone back on the plinth whilst the other hit the big marshmallow button, soft so you didn't get hurt in the excitement; the scream of the siren woke even the dumbo sleepers. They would be straining the bounds of earth before the sun set in the highland mist. The Royal Air Force was once again offering a hand of life to some poor climbers.

Alex picked up his large rucksack, climbing boots, ice pick and cold weather clothing. He had been climbing since going to St. Andrew's University. He loved his home grown Highlands, the thrill of straining his body with every crampon foot on the ice sheet. He enjoyed working for Price Waterhouse in Edinburgh, making his sums add up and forecasting the future for the large investments he was controlling. He led a comfortable life style, picking up a very large reward for his responsibility. It was in his nature to gamble, but like a racing driver he was very thorough with his risk assessment. He was looking forward to climbing in the historical pass through which the river Garry flowed. The mountains on either side towered above the road corralling the pass below: the site of a famous Jacobean battle in 1689. He wore a silver cross around his neck which he never took off. It was at church that he had met Laura; she was singing in the church choir. She had become an appendage, not a partner, but a close companion and climber.

Laura hauled up the blanket and folded it into the small space available. The blanket, a development from the space race, was silver, light and very warm, better than any water bottle when she was screwed up in a snow hole. She glowed in anticipation of the climbing promised that Saturday. Alex was so competent she had no worries about her safety; she valued his leadership and a few hugs but she hated being frozen. She wore a size twelve, so average build, had glistening red hair, bright green icicle eyes and intoxicating strength. Her degree was a long slog, but her skills as an urologist had been a bonus to Aberdeen hospital. Her boss Professor Bloom was keen to come along, he had climbed the Himalayas so always felt that climbing in Scotland was a step down. He would enjoy a weekend with her despite the fact she never stopped talking about her friend Alex. At least he would be roped up to her for a few hours.

Robert Bloom slid into his narrow trousers and light weight clothing. He added a few more layers of clothing, always the best way to dress for climbing in the bitter cold of Scotland. He had found his miner's light; strapped round his head it was always useful to be able to work with both hands when he had to climb at night. He was hoping that would be the last thing they would be doing. He was looking forward to a relaxing Saturday night in a Sgian-dubh pub somewhere.

They arrived separately meeting in the car park in the middle of the pass. Alex was prepared with the latest weather forecast and a climbing plan. The weather would be good for most of the day, cold keeping the snow in place, with a slight possibly of becoming overcast giving a fall of sleet or snow; that was the forecast for the afternoon. They should be on the way down by then so no worries.

Alex greeted Laura with a close warming hug and a cold handed hand shake with Bloom. The sky was just lighting up but the black sided mountains made a witches cavern look inviting. His footstep cracked the ice puddle as he led the small party to the base of the first pitch. Bloom had trickles of sweat seeping into his armpits. Occasionally gulping air he climbed with purpose determined to keep up with the other two. He was reminding himself that Everest was a lot higher than this and he had made it; well half way. He would not tell them he had to be escorted down.

Laura glowed. She was close to Alex but not yet roped up and had no breath left to speak, just an understanding. She had a slight niggle that Robert lagged but looking round she saw him there. He flashed her a wide grin which was not reciprocated. They had a mountain to climb and energy had to be reserved.

The shadow moved from the peaks and began to brighten up the valley. They had reached the pitch where they were to rope up and attach their crampons. Their feet sank gushingly into the snow, softly, whooshing like pistons, except that it was a very slow steam engine. An apparent line of rabbit droppings followed them, but there were no rabbits only boot steps. They climbed higher and although the sun was now visible, a sharp shadow was just above them, it was getting colder and the virgin snow was becoming sharper. Alex shouted,

'Watch for any movement of the snow, there could be a few

holes and a crevasse or two. This is not a normal snow state so please ensure your rope is tight and secure.'

They both nodded and came to a stop. Robert glowed and breathed a little easier. Laura took the rope from Alex, catching a glint in his eyes, a trace of apprehension crossed his forehead, which cooled her ardour and replaced it with concern. She passed the rope to Robert without a word. He took it and wound it around his waist; a figure of eight done without a murmur. They were now high enough to sense the silence. Laura looked up into the sheen of white. Sunglasses had little effect but she could see enough in front of her to follow Alex's trail. She glanced down the valley which was now bathed in a sharp light. There was a maculated edge to the snow, some patches of green and a grey thread of road far below, which cobbled the scene together.

Her mind drifted. She could easily move down to Edinburgh and get a good job in the hospital. She would see more of Alex and Murrayfield, a Mecca for rugby. Her plan to be closer would give him an opportunity; so no more excuses. He could take her to watch the rugby matches and there was that lovely old castle by the Forth Bridge where they did weddings in the keep. She knew it could only accommodate about thirty people so who would they invite? Could his mother climb the circular staircase? It was very narrow. The thought of her white dress brought her back to reality; the climb was becoming very steep.

A tug on the rope and she whipped round to see Robert struggling. He waved at her to carry on. Alex began to slow too. Her chest was heaving, clamped and hot she struggled with uncomfortable thoughts. Alex had his ice pick probing the snow, which was becoming increasingly heavy. Again the rope strained from behind. 'Oh! Robert do keep up', she thought, but was more concerned that Alex was not looking normal, more crouched, probing. And then he had gone. She was catapulted forward, nearly cut in two by the force from behind and then she hit the survival button, heels dug in, ice pick thrown out to the side and grasping it with both hands she prayed. Robert was doing the same but he was not so alert so he was rewarded by crashing, full bodied into Laura. They froze, both holding the rope which was taut down to a point about five yards ahead of them which then disappeared into the snow. Aphony. It was awhile before Laura was able to create a sound.

'Alex are you alright?'

'Yes, I am in a crevasse. I will try and climb out but I think I may have dislocated my leg. Be careful when you pull on the rope. I am concerned the snow may have been dislodged and could cause an avalanche.'

Laura held her breath. She was screwed up like a road jack, was she to screw up or down? She prayed.

'Laura get stuck in and make yourself fast. God will help you but you must help yourself too. We will have to pull Alex out slowly and quietly. The snow feels very unstable. Can you use your phone and call for assistance immediately. It sounds as if Alex has a broken leg? '

They secured their ice axes and attached the end of the rope. Creeping forward like an Arctic fox they reached the gaping hole. There was Alex, a pendulum in space, his leg at a very funny angle. As Robert moved forward Laura noticed the shadow on the other side of the valley. The sun had passed its zenith. She called the emergency service.

'Oh! Hell, what have I done?', thought Alex.

'I am here dangling like a corpse without a noose. Thank

goodness the rope is holding. I hope Laura can hold it. I should have been more careful. Why did I come today? It was Laura, she is a lovely woman and I wanted to be with her, but she had to bring her bloody boss. I only hope he is going to pull his weight. I cannot feel my feet. The excruciating pain in my right leg feels as if it's badly twisted or broken. Dam. What a mess. What lengths do I go to, just to be with her? He relaxed and let his mind wander. I should be having tea by the fire on a day like this. When I get off this mountain I must say something to Laura. Aberdeen is a bit far so perhaps I can persuade her to come to Edinburgh. Oh! Let's get on with it, my hands are turning blue. It's a long drop if they run out of strength. Thank the Lord they are hauling me up.'

Robert and Laura began pulling at the rope. Alex helped by clawing at the side of the icy well until inch by inch the rope began to ooze back onto the snow. It took a long time. The shadows were now half way down the side of the southern slope. Egressing Alex from the hole, yelping with pain as his leg came over the rim, Robert secured him onto his space blanket.

'Laura please confirm you have alerted the emergency services.' Robert grew in confidence, he had taken charge. Laura confirmed she had contacted them but she would call them again. She too was feeling more confident in their situation.

'We are on the North face of the Killiecrankie pass about five hundred feet up ... Yes we are a party of three. One male has fallen through a crevasse and broken his leg. We need assistance. We will try and make ourselves more visible but be advised we are worried that the snow is melting and the surface is becoming unstable.'

Her hands were shaking. She realised that to help Alex she had to use the pick embedded in the snow. Robert heaved, threw a rope around the pick and pulled. It gave way. Laura used her scarf and used the pick to secure a splint to Alex's leg. Robert meanwhile had set up the stove and was making a brew; he also had some soup in a self heating can. After Alex had had his soup and tasted the much sweetened tea, his cheeks began to change from deathly white to pale pink. Robert hadn't been on Everest for nothing, he knew his priorities. It was turning very cold and in the valley the grey ribbon was now black with points of scumbled lights appearing in the car park. They hoped they would be rescued soon. Robert looked at his right arm, spit, spot, spit, drummed the precipitation. They pulled their hoods closer to their heads and covered Alex in any spare covering they could find. They must keep him awake. Laura knew they couldn't give him any pills until he had been examined. She felt cold and nauseous. Why was she here? Climbing had never been like this before. Her eyes closed, her brain stopped. Was this the kismet moment?

The sound of the Sea King's clattering blades filled the sky. They could see the lights in the mackerel sky. The sky was falling. Laura rang the Rescue Centre again to say they had spotted the helicopter. She was told to keep her phone activated as it would help the helicopter crew locate their position.

'Be advised the snow is very wet and an avalanche is possible.'

They were spotted; the aircraft made a slow lazy turn overhead and then turned away to become a blob on the far horizon. Robert and Laura hugged; they watched as the helicopter lined up to face them head on although it was still some miles away. There was blackness in the valley and it was creeping up to them. They thought they saw a fly below the helicopter, but soon realised it was a stretcher. Down it came with the crewman. He settled in the snow some feet before them. The stretcher which hung from the wire snake remained still whilst the wire weaved from side to side disappearing into the fading gloom, high up to the noisy beast. Pulling the stretcher towards them they all managed to manoeuvre Alex into the wire basket. The crewman explained that the helicopter was in a very high hover as not to disturb the snow and cause an avalanche. He assured them that once Alex was on board he would be in good hands and taken directly to the local hospital. They hoped so.

Alex went up; the basket disappeared to be digested by the yellow buzzing bee. The helicopter remained static. Then the crewman was winched down again. Suddenly he was with them with two harnesses plus a big bag for all their equipment. They stuffed all their supplies into the big brown bag. He made sure they were secure before they were lifted into the night sky to join their injured colleague. They both realised Alex was now very secure and that they had been rescued just in time before the blanket of night had covered them.

The survivors were surprised at the noise and the vibration of the helicopter as they remained wrapped in their own thoughts. They were just becoming comatose when the aircrafts noise changed pitch and with a bump landed. The big door opened to reveal an ambulance which would take them to the main entrance of the hospital. They were loaded into the ambulance but before the hour hand reached five they had disembarked; Alex was whisked away to the operating theatre.

Robert was reticent. He was still white, his eyes unfocused, he was still seeing mountains from the past but he stood differently, more upright and secure. The day had been an epiphany for him. Laura was comfortably warmer which left her mind freer. She was happy and grateful that the rescue had been so swift and successful. She waited patiently for the news of Alex. His big strong frame had been crumpled and he could not speak very clearly as he had been in deep shock but there was no frost bite. She prayed that his leg was a simple fracture and that he would not suffer from any permanent damage. As long as his brain and fingers were working he could do his job. Her thoughts turned to the men who had shared her memorable day. Robert had certainly shone in a different light and she saw him differently. He had proved that he could be more gentle and considerate; she had no idea of what had happened to his mind but something had changed. She now looked forward to working with him again. As for Alex, she smiled and felt a glow, she realised what she had to do; a move to Edinburgh was still the plan.

Coddle Soup

Frank had found the Garden of Remembrance, up the hill not far from O'Connell Street in Dublin. It was built for those Irish who had fallen in the fight for Ireland's independence. He climbed the steps on that silent morning, it was quiet, no rain, wind but a dull mist hung over the city. There were no names carved on the curved stone but there was a terrific French poem – La Vision. It had taken him an age to translate, before realising the English version was below. It was written in a similar way but it was not the same. The French was so much more emotional.

He crossed Parnell Square North and entered the Writer's Museum. There was a lot to absorb from Swift to Behan. There were actual writings, splendid busts and death masks but no tea. He left the museum after an hour, parched, turned right and saw a flashing walking figure in lights, inviting the public to visit the Dublin City Gallery and Tea Room. Just what he needed, the entrance was free.

He entered the gallery, missed what was on the wall as he made for the Tea Room. The tea was made from very soft water and went down a treat. The same water source was used in the production of the local Guinness, another delight. He was soon refreshed and made to leave the gallery. He noticed that some of the painters exhibiting included Monet, Manet and Francis Bacon. Bacon was one of his favourites; he had been awed by the slurred cinematographic features of brilliantly coloured slewed faces. That was in the Birmingham Art Gallery years ago when he was at the Art College. He had to see these latest canvases. Frank noted that they were at the back of the gallery, down the long hall. Strolling along the long passageway he was aware of the beautiful atmospheric Monets and Manets hung on either side, such a contrast to the screaming renditions by Bacon.

Admiring Bacon's contribution he struck up a conversation with one of the museum statuesque attendants standing close to a violently coloured Bacon canvas.

'Yes, I met Bacon's sister once, she lived in South Africa, sadly she died a couple of years ago,' said the man. He was a young looking middle aged dark haired Irishman, with dark brown eyes, a snub nose and willowy hands. He told Frank that he had been in the museum service for thirty five years.

'I have met a few celebrities in my time', he admitted. 'One day I saw a large, obviously American, fella with a beautiful young girl. She looked completely out of place.'

The girl approached our attendant and asked him how she could make coddle soup? Taken aback, he told her how to make it and where to purchase the ingredients in Dublin. She wasn't interested.

'I wanna make it when I get back to New York,' drawled the girl.

'No way!' said the attendant, 'all the ingredients will have gone off by the time you get home'.

'Do you know who my man is?' The attendant shook his head but she ignored his ignorance. 'I wanna photo of you both'

The attendant obliged standing side by side and then posed shaking hands with the large American stranger. Once the photographs had been taken the strangers left without even looking at the paintings.

Weeks passed when one morning the Director of the gallery sent for my attendant acquaintance.

'Well Sean, I never realised you knew famous people'

'I don't,' replied the quietly spoken attendant.

'Sean, this morning I have received a wonderful letter from New York from a well known film director who is full of your praise. Do you know who I mean?'

'No! But a few weeks ago I did meet a couple who asked me how to make coddle soup, and then asked me to pose for some photos.'

'Didn't you tell them about our gallery and our wonderful exhibits?'

'No, I'm sorry; I just told them how to make the soup and where to get the ingredients'. He now realised he should have possibly told them more about the gallery.

'I can tell you Sean, Oliver Stone thinks you're just fantastic,' beamed the Director.

'Well done! He has enclosed a photo of you and him with a comment on the back, "Coddle soup made for dinner party, no takers," does that make any sense? '

The attendant had told Frank the story in a very matter of fact, rambling sort of way.

'What is coddle soup?' Frank asked the attendant. 'It sounds good.'

'The Dublin version is full of vegetables, sausages, cooked ham, and thyme leaves,' sighed the attendant, he obviously had told many more how to make the soup, 'and make sure you boil it long and slow, best served with buttered soda bread.'

Frank made a note to ensure that he made it as per the recipe.

'I could also tell you about Heather McCartney, when she and Paul came to a showing,'

'Thanks Sean, but no, I have to catch the City bus. It's waiting outside'.

Frank left the quiet Irishman, wondering what other jewels the attendant could have told him. However he had a secret recipe and he would certainly remember the Irish attendant as he sipped his coddle soup.

       *   *   *

Frank was having his car washed when he met Colin, a

Dubliner. He recounted the story but said he never really knew what coddle soup was.

'Well it's Dublin Coddle Soup that yer after', grinned Colin, 'I make it here in Mablethorpe with pieces of gammon from the butcher in Skegness, but lardons will do. Add some small sausages, carrots, onions and greens. Twenty minutes before serving put in the potatoes, keep stirring and serve. That's coddle soup.'

Now you know, so you too can serve up this tasty soup!

An African Encounter

Africa is a gigantic continent; it has millions of people from different tribes with many traditions, creeds and political persuasions. It harbours some of the richest minerals in the world which historically has attracted many world powers. A Reuters' correspondent, who lived in Cape Town, South Africa, was once asked to cover a war in Chad by his London office. He replied, 'You cover it, you are closer!' Such is the length of Africa. With such an array of riches the area is governed by a variety of leaders, all craving power. This is a story which concerns a small incident which could have had catastrophic consequences.

The bright searing sun burnt his face. Public school and Army trained, David Armstrong, a six foot, dark haired, swarthy skinned pilot had only recently flown into Kinshasa. The previous six months he had been with an expedition. He looked towards the city which was dominated by black, purple grey and white clouds which were building rapidly. He knew he had to get on before the precipitation of slashing rain and floods made his journey impossible. David had to make the monthly appointment; he threw his two bags into the four by four. The African driver was revving the vehicle aware of the impending change in the weather. They were perspiring profusely and beginning to reek with the smell of well worn socks; but that was unnoticeable in the swamp of other odious matter left in the road. The vehicle raced off into the city, down the wide arterial road enclosed on both sides with hoardings.

Elephants in the Bush

'Welcome to Ali and Foreman', the words were large and inviting. The hoardings were painted in red, green and black, the national colours of the country. 'The rumble in the jungle' was going to take place that Saturday in the large football arena: it had caught the imagination of the boxing world. The hoardings hid the slums of shacks and corrugated iron dens. The wagon slowed, the driver began frantically tooting the horn, David clasped his hands; time was passing.

The expedition had arrived from the United Kingdom to explore and circumnavigate the Zaire River, now known as the Congo. It was made up of mainly British Army personnel but had experts from all disciplines. The support aircraft had a single engine and seats for six people; David was the only pilot. The aircraft had the ability to land and take off from short unprepared jungle strips. The flying was hazardous in such a vast country with little communications and changeable weather. In the course of time he had been made aware of the political problems but now arriving in the city, he sensed he had entered a powder keg. The American Embassy was his refuge: his ally was the American Air Attaché, an Army Colonel. The driver's knowledge of the city enabled them to arrive with minutes to spare.

'Hi David, what have you brought in today?' the pasty faced Colonel greeted him warmly.

'Just some photos of a jet landing at a strip out East. I don't think it's anything special.' The Colonel grabbed the photographs; his eyes widened but said nothing.

'I am sorry I shall have to leave you in my secretary's capable hands. Please can you leave the rest of your report with her?' He picked up his papers and left. David was taken aback, his features remained frozen. There were things that he could not reveal to her, not even the British Ambassador knew the relationship he had with the American. The attractive American woman extended a lithesome hand, 'Hi, I'm Laura Ford, so you are the handsome British pilot we have all heard about'. David saw no flicker in her eyes. Her look was lancinating, enough to burn through him but he was not going to say anything that was politically sensitive. Nevertheless he felt exposed. She was too sharp in her questioning; she could be CIA. He gave her a short report, then made his excuses and left. He reached for the door but was prevented by the onrush of a smart, well figured blonde who stood just below his shoulder level. Their eyes held, within a second she blurted, 'Hi! You are the new pilot in town. I am hosting a party on Sunday, would you like to come?' Laura introduced this tornado as the American Ambassador's daughter. He rose like a lion to admire his lioness.

David taken aback quietly replied, 'Thanks, I shall be there!'

He slept like Morpheus, to be woken by a call from the British Ambassador. He asked David if he would take him for a joy ride to see the sites. Sunday was the only day he was free. David immediately agreed realising that it would be an early start before the party. Early Sunday morning David picked up the Ambassador in a borrowed Renault; sadly it managed to break down just as the Embassy gates closed behind them. Opposite the British Embassy, across the square, was the Russian Embassy. Scenes of the Ambassador pushing an old car to get it started, on a Sunday morning, must have confused the Russians. They boarded the aircraft in Ndolo, the airfield in town. The Ambassador told David where to fly and soon they found a large tented camp. 'Down there is a Chinese training camp kept secret from all except the President, Mbuto Seko Seko. He knows about this place', the Ambassador purred.

That night David reacquainted himself with the party host. She was attentive all night and by the end of the evening they had become close. They arranged to meet again the following evening,

Next day he relaxed before picking up his American beauty.

It was after dinner in the 'Intercontinental Hotel' that she suggested they had coffee at home. David was reticent, but he agreed, perhaps he was too nervous and was sensing intrigue everywhere. She gripped his hand and pressed her curved body into his compressed chest. Arriving at the Embassy the thick iron doors clanked behind them. Helping the young lady down from her wagon he glimpsed at the Marine in the shadows, his muscles tensed. The door opened and he was absorbed into the atmosphere of silence, charm and America. The interior of the Embassy was striking with opulent furnishings, big and bold. He settled into the deep settee, his host sat close but suddenly jumped up as the door opened. David stood but his space was invaded by the musk aroma of a long legged, long haired, middle-aged, multi- lined woman who closed in on him. He took a step backward.

'Please sit, I am so pleased to meet you, I am the Ambassador's wife. A British pilot in these parts is so remarkable, you are very welcome; I hope you are going to stay awhile.' David sighed, her body language was far too forward for him to cope with; her daughter had been kinder, his mouth dried?

'I am pleased to meet you; you make me feel so welcome'.

The conversation continued until he heard a scuffling from outside the door. Footsteps ran down some stairs then disappeared; the rhythm was unusual, not American feet. Both women looked alarmed and the mother excused herself and left. The daughter's mood changed, she came closer, her voice was deeper and quieter, nearly a whisper, 'David I have a great favour to ask but it is a matter of life and death'. David's mind suddenly saw a number of scenarios. He immediately realised it was his skill as a pilot and his sturdy plane they wanted.

David felt the ants crawling down the back of his neck, he wanted to scratch and scream at the same time. He had entered the maelstrom, and he kicked himself inwardly, he knew that there was no going back and he had to remain calm and swim in the flow. The British phlegmatic stance would save the day, he held onto that belief. He let her explain.

'We are harbouring a Prime Minister, his wife and two children. My father is unaware of them, if he was he would immediately hand them over to the authorities. Mother and I are praying that you will agree to fly them out! Please will you help us David? '

Well the cards were now on the table; he had a decision

to make. Upset and corralled he had no reason to stay. He felt comforted that he had planned to fly home in the next few days, but they would know that. He told the hovering woman that he would call her the next day. He was escorted out. Alone and weary, he drove back to his apartment.

The aircraft engineers were carrying out an inspection prior to the long flight to England. Parked in the very hot sun, they found it difficult to touch the boiling screws as they fixed the aircraft panels. They were enclosed in a sticky cocoon. Suddenly the aircraft was surrounded by khaki coloured vehicles, men with weapons and a big broad set officer who set about checking the interior of the aircraft. The engineers looked on in silence. Nothing was found so the vehicles were started and the soldiers disappeared. The engineers were unsure about this action; whatever it was, they were frightened. David appeared through the haze. He would do the test flight on Saturday afternoon. He joked that at least the emergency services would be available as there were so few aircraft take offs and landings on Saturdays.

He called her at the Embassy to arrange another meeting. She met him at the 'Inter Continental' for lunch. She had booked a room for 'afters' to give him all the details and to show her appreciation. Their smiles and close embrace as they left was typical of a pair of young, exhausted lovers. David was now committed.

It was a lie that the fugitive in the American Embassy was a Prime Minister but he was a very important politician who had opposed the Government. He was from the eastern side of the country where thousands of his people had died. He had decided to seek refuge in a more understanding democratic country, the United States. Once he arrived at the American Embassy he was made aware of the Ambassador's opposition to harbouring any political refugees. He knew that had he been handed over to the President's men, he and his family would be massacred. It was fortunate that the first person he met was the Ambassador's wife. Once she realised his plight she had hidden him and his family. She confided in her daughter with the situation. It was the daughter who had found a possible solution, a young British pilot; so David was now totally involved. David began formulating his plans, one where he had to trust his engineers. He was well aware of the risk to himself but most of all to his Government. He could not fail with the escape plan.

Saturday dawned with a bright blue sky, a day after a tropical storm of bucketing rain and lightning, a pattern found on the Equator. The sun climbed and with it the temperature, shadows that were not there as the sun was always directly above you in that part of Africa. Dressing for a judgement day, David drew up his lightweight flying suit and desert boots. Soft to the touch, sandy coloured with rubber soles and thick laces. Wearing dark glasses, which were essential, he boarded his Land Rover, throwing in his bag with minimum kit. The adventure had begun.

Arriving in Ndolo he greeted his crew. They had fitted the four seats in the back, filled the tanks and had given the aircraft a full inspection. It now needed an air test but there was no time, David put his trust in his skilled engineers to have it all tight and secure. The second hands of clocks moved on, the minutes moved and the hour came. Not too early as he needed just enough daylight to get to his destination. One foot on the step, a hand on the door and he swung himself into the seat. The chief engineer stood, level with the cockpit floor awaiting the order to start. Parched mouths and lips seeking the trickling sweat from their faces was the only indication that the tension was in their guts.

'Clear prop, magnetos set, contact!' The order thundered across the silent apron. They had gambled that there would only be a few aircraft moving that afternoon, besides thunderstorms normally started at four so most aircraft departed in the morning. The engine burst into life, clouds of black smoke, burning off the new oil, the noise became a roar; a deep cavernous roar, not like a motorbike more like an elephant thundering after its prey. David touched the throttle and called for clearance from air traffic control. Permission granted he rolled the sixty foot wing spanned aircraft slowly forward. A touch on the brake slewed the aircraft to one side; it was not a maintenance fault but planned. At that moment a large black smoked screened vehicle came close to the right wing, four people leapt out and ran towards the opened aircraft door. Someone threw them in. It was all over within a few seconds and he was taxiing again. He smelt the frightened bodies that were now clinging to the floor, as briefed. Without stopping he did the aircraft checks prior to take off, the taxi way was long so he had time. There was no alarm from air traffic when he requested permission to take off. Keeping the aircraft rolling onto the runway he thrust the throttle fully forward, gathering speed, the air was hot and the runway long and then the lightning of a load, with wheels still rumbling the ground eased away. A gentle turn towards the river, climbing for the nearest cloud and they were soon over the border. He knew that there were no fighters in Brazzaville to worry about but there may be some further en route. The aircraft was kept at a low level, hugging the few cumulus clouds that were beginning to build. The passengers clambered into their seats and grabbed the sick bags; it was a roller coaster ride.

Some three hours later David spotted the long black strip at Libreville. After landing he taxied slowly towards the apron which was about a mile away. A large van crashed out of the jungle, doors opened and a man frantically waved for the aircraft to stop. The passengers needed no encouragement, the aircraft door was swung open and they were gone. The van disappeared back into the jungle. David moved the aircraft on and entered the apron. There was just one marshaller. It was dusk so the rest must have gone home. He filed his flight plan for Port Harcourt, Nigeria, for the next day. The clerk made no comment that he had just flown in without one.

His flight to Port Harcourt was uneventful. On arrival he rolled to a stop and was surrounded by military armed trucks. His jawed dropped and he felt his muscles tense. Slowly undoing his straps he released the door and then slid to the ground. He looked up and saw that the Nigerians had big wide toothy grins; they parted to allow a typical Foreign Office chap approach the aircraft. He was dressed in crisp bright white trousers, an Oxford blue shirt with regimental tie and that universal British Panama hat.

His hand was suddenly thrust forward,

'Well done you have achieved an amazing coup, the Americans are very grateful'.

His knees nearly gave way, followed by an expelling of air from pent up lungs. He was now content knowing that his passengers were safe, wherever they were. His thoughts crystallised as he reflected on a conversation that he had had with his Dutch friend in Kinshasa. They had been discussing Patrice Lumumba, a leader of a breakaway province of the Congo in the 60s, later Zaire. In the early 70s, the Dutchman had been working in the province's capital, Limumbashi, a town five hundred miles from Kinshasa. One day, on his way to work, his taxi driver had shown him the place where Lumumba had been assassinated. Many people in Zaire thought it was the work of the CIA. David knew better, Lumumba had not been killed by the Americans as they had been scared of the consequences. He had heard that a British woman working for the British Intelligence services was not so concerned; she had made sure the deed was done. Was this another American favour to be returned later?

The Greyhound Bus Ride

Have you ever thought of travelling by bus in the United States? It is possibly a consideration only when you can't get somewhere by normal means. Then the world will tell you 'Take the Greyhound'. At this point you are unaware that 95 percent of the indigenous population of the United States has never stepped on a bus, but they know the Greyhound. Myths perpetuated by films, plays or television series, enable those who believe in them, to reassure you of what to expect. There is the big unique bus to somewhere. They say it with no thought but it's accepted that it is the answer to every connection that can't be made by car, plane or train. America's finest and most well know bus company, the Greyhound, has tentacles spread all over the United States. This is a story to read first before hauling you and your bag aboard; you may want to reconsider or it might whet your appetite for an adventure.

*   *   *

James was supposed to have flown to Nashville but he had received a phone call from his sister advising him that the weather forecast was poor. It was the first phone call that he had ever received from her where she had shown concern about the weather so he decided to look at the weather picture himself.

He had been in the United States for nearly a week, having flown from Birmingham UK, to Atlanta via Paris then on to Fort Myers. There he had been picked up by his long standing friends Dick and Marge. They had first met many years ago and had been to his place in France. They drove for the hour long trip to Marco Island where he had been invited to stay in their 'condo' for a week. Their 'condo' or apartment was on the idyllic island of Marco in SW Florida. Marco Island is an expensive gem in the USA where many of the rich fly down to in the winter, and where some who love it, stay there.

His sister and her husband would find it difficult to reach Nashville airport as tornadoes, thunderstorms and flooding were forecast. He reviewed the weather radar pictures on the TV and quickly realised she was so right to be concerned. The red and yellow paint strip which ran south west to north east in Tennessee spelt out the situation. As a retired airline pilot of many years he knew what the picture meant – strong turbulence, heavy rains, violent winds, hail, lightning and buckets of rain. Not for him, he picked up the phone and cancelled the flights.

The forecast was correct. In Nashville an annual rain fall fell in twenty four hours, they had had a series of tornadoes and thousands were made homeless, even the Grand Ol' Oprey was flooded and amongst other things many famous guitars were destroyed.

James looked at the alternatives: his options were to hire a car and drive the long journey or be driven and travel by the Greyhound bus service. The Greyhound could be an experience to savour. He had grown up seeing films of people crossing the USA on the Greyhound, read about it and had heard stories of 'gap year' students who had used the service. He resolved that it was an opportunity not to be missed. Dick was a little sceptical. One of his sons had ridden the bus whilst at college and was not impressed; James' sister, who had lived in Tennessee for over forty years, had never taken the ride. He felt he had nothing to lose.

His friends took him to Naples on a Wednesday in May and pulled into the small bus station. It was managed by a kindly guy, Russ Hartland. He was happy to answer all their questions and sold him a 'seniors' ticket to Murfreesboro in Tennessee. The cost was just $135 for a distance of over 950 miles. Whilst they waited he told them some history of the Greyhound bus service which had originated when a man using an old truck had begun taking friends and neighbours into town. A bus company was formed, more companies were taken over and absorbed and developed into the empire it is today with a multitude of bus routes served by the famous Greyhound buses.

The flight that he had initially booked would have cost about $240 to transfer to another flight; the same price that it had cost him to cross the Atlantic, without taxes. No wonder people think twice about flying to the USA and feel cheated when due to unforeseen circumstances they have to change their plans. He recalled the time when he was in Sydney, Australia and had to change his 'round the world ticket', then it only cost A$25!

The bus arrived on schedule. The Greyhound bus was about thirty feet long, had six large wheels with a long large leaping greyhound logo on each side. It was a good step up into the bus, had rows of comfortable looking blue seats which were wide and a 'restroom' in the rear. The driver sat in a cabin, where he was protected by a solid plastic sheet at his back which stretched from floor to ceiling and a large door that could be swung out into the aisle. It was bolted whilst moving to prevent anyone interfering with the driver. The driving panel had all the normal gauges plus a computer which was used for the ticketing and journey details.

His suitcase was loaded and he was soon aboard waving goodbye to his dear friends. There were only about ten people dotted about the bus. They were a mixture of tourists and commuters, mainly black or brown; he curled into his seat, he was the white man. They were dressed in poor lightweight clothing, dull colours for Americans and generally hatted with the universal base ball hat or 'hoody'. The dark blue seats were comfortable and he had no problem stretching his legs. His ticket said that there were seven stops to Murfreesboro, his destination in Tennessee. Little did he realise that they didn't have enough paper to print out all the stops!

The driver was black, called Eddie Floyd. This was printed on his name tag. He did the standard announcements. It didn't take long for him to feel relaxed knowing that he had a competent driver. They drove off passing lines of palm trees, a variety of new buildings and following parallel canals and lakes which were on either side of the highway. They were heading for the I 75. The main highways in the States were designated International, I. He was absorbed, looking for alligators and iguanas. Iguanas, large long lizards normally kept to the Florida Everglades, a swamp area. James had heard on the local Florida news that many iguanas had become displaced due to the very cold winter and had moved from the swamps to warmer places like houses, cafes, restaurants and roads. He didn't manage to see any. There were an incredible number of cars, trucks and recreational vehicles (RVs) heading north along the highway. It was obviously the summer exodus for the Florida inhabitants looking for cooler climes of the North. One trailer held a vehicle with a large three bladed propeller, it surged ahead, an airboat similar to those seen on the Everglades. It surely would be of little use in Illinois. That was followed by a trail of large long 'semi's, they were either towing or carrying cars. 'Semis' were grander, longer and bigger than any trailer lorries seen in Europe. 'Semis' were 'Artics' in another language, English. The speed limit on the highway was 70mph which applied equally to cars as well as those big heavy trucks and semis.

An hour later they were pulling in to Fort Myers. Here was a neatly laid out terminus with fourteen anxious people waiting to board the bus. Soft bags were the order of the day. How many would board? There were no surf boards and everyone appeared to be wearing brighter summer clothes. Perhaps they were on vacation and less travelled than the passengers they were about to join. The driver loaded the bags, collected the tickets and they were off again. The passengers were a mixture of Hispanics, poorly dressed white people and blacks anxious to find a seat. There were no assigned seats so it was a case of first come, first served. A pit stop and soon off again at 1205 for Puenta Gorda where they arrived at 1220 and departed at 12.30. On arrival they had been warned by the driver not to leave the bus for any reason; those that smoke would have to hang on! A gallon of diesel and gas, petrol, were advertised at $3.30 and $2.86. What a revelation, a gallon of British diesel which is 4.56 litres rather than 4.0 litres in the USA, costs $8.7. He thought that Americans should be grateful for such cheap fuel. Later he noticed that at Arby's restaurant, a popular highway restaurant chain, a pint of lime and lemonade cost $3.60; more expensive than a gallon of fuel.

The sun was streaming through the windows; the air conditioning was becoming a bonus as the outside temperature climbed into the 90s. The bus was tracking up the West coast of Florida route bombarded by sun, sun, sun all the way, the road shimmered but the bus remained reasonably cool. On the driver's panel the temperature was hovering around 70F, quite comfortable.

Flags fluttered limply, sailing boats meandered out at sea and birds hung onto the light thermals as they looked for fish. Onwards they drove turning to the north east.

Next stop Braderton. A flashing sign some fifteen feet high on the side of the road said 85F then dialled up WELCOME MISSY – It was Mother's day on Sunday. Two men disembarked at the Braderton depot, a simple brick building. More cases and packages erupted from the place. The town looked no different from the others they had passed through. Bungalows lined the route, they all had white fences and were surrounded with wide porches; some had large rocking chairs or swings sitting solidly in the shadows. The occasional old air conditioning unit was left swinging from a window. This was a warm May, how would the occupants cope in July? The bus left the US 41. The two men who had disembarked had to wait for their onward transport in the blazing heat; there were no seats at this depot. Several ladies, dressed in bright loud colours, followed by a big beefy chap, boarded the bus. How was he going to fit into his seat despite the fact that the Greyhound bus seat was larger than a regular bus seat? The doors closed, the bus pulled out just after two thirty.

He looked around and surveyed the bus. He realised that he had joined another strata of American society. People were travelling in all sorts of clothes, jeans, vests, skirts, dresses, open necked shirts and neckerchiefs. Generally old or middle aged, some children but no youths, they had other things to do beside travel. They all looked reasonably clean, no nose twitching or nausea, an agreeable odour, they were all washed. James sat back and thought about this bus; this bus was a cut above other buses that he had travelled on in other parts of the world; the West Indies, Africa and Arabia. No crush, nothing loaded on the roof and no animals running around the passengers, no chickens. Above all there was a very competent driver conducting his bus along the highways, sometimes in very heavy traffic, and sometimes through narrowed lanes at road works and city congested lines. The smooth gear changes and a workable air conditioning unit made the journey so pleasant; James was so relaxed he dozed.

They were heading for St. Petersburg, a town between Tampa Bay and the Gulf of Mexico known locally as St. Pete; it was founded in about 1888. The road split a large expanse of water. Ahead of the fast travelling bus was a very long, high and aesthetic looking suspension bridge. The 'Greyhound' climbed steeply, slowly decelerating as it reached the zenith of the bridge; below following in the water was a large white sailed yacht which was heeled hard over. The strong wind blew the swift craft to pass under the bridge. A large truck, a semi, accelerated past the big bus only to slow up as it reached the summit and braked hard ahead of them as it accelerated down the steep slope on the other side of the bridge. They were soon on the mainland of St. Petersburg and driving into the city centre. The city had been named after its namesake in Russia as the founder of St. Pete, Peter Demens, had spent half his youth there. Known as the 'Sunshine City' it has the Guinness World Record for logging the most consecutive days of sunshine – 768! It has a low cost of living and with the long days of sunshine, there is little wonder that it is a popular retirement destination, although recently it is moving into a more youthful direction.

The bus had hardly stopped in the terminal before the smoked starved passengers were bundling off the bus in order to puff in the bright sunlight; they were soon dragging on their weeds. The embarking passengers waited patiently. An old man with a long hair and a matted beard sat cross legged on the sun drenched bench, he was wearing military fatigues. He peered through his dark glasses as he held his metal walking stick. James wondered if he was going to board the bus but he sat statuesqued leaving all the other travellers to pass by. Did he know where he was going to or was he waiting for someone? The bus throbbed and slowly moved forward; no one ever knew his fate. He was still there as they headed out of the terminal for Clearwater.

St. Petersburg, a modern town was full of life with lots of freshly painted houses was passing but no time to linger. Within the bus there was a change of atmosphere; there was grumbling in the back and complaints could be heard that it was becoming hot, perhaps it was an air conditioning system failure that could only be felt at the rear of the bus, the front was fine. Soon they were travelling on a long causeway; palm trees were dotted either side of the road as blue water rolled in across the beaches. Above them, hanging on wires, was a big green sign that announced the city of Tampa. A modern city began to unfold. Suddenly a large imposing building appeared on the left hand side of the road. SHRINER HQ said the plaque on the wall. At the front of the building was a large fountain along with the statue of a tall man with a fez, cradling a young boy in his arms. It was certainly an imposing statue. Was this the Shriner Company that James had heard about in the Middle East and Africa?

Tampa had been explored by the Spanish in the 16th Century, who brought with them European diseases which harmed the native population. It had initially been called Fort Brooke in 1849 but began to expand with the arrival of the railroad in the 1880's when its name was changed to Tampa. Phosphates were discovered and the town expanded rapidly supplemented by the new cigar manufacturing industry. They were approaching the bus terminal of America's fifth most popular and wealthy city which suffers from regular summer storms and accompanying lightning strikes. It certainly looked a bright, clean and respectable place. They drove into downtown, the city centre, to find the bus terminal which was small for the size of city; it only had ten berths. Inside the terminal there were seats for about a quarter of the passengers as all the buses appeared to be travelling full. On arrival the passengers were informed they had to disembark and change buses; the complaints from the people in the rear had been noted. The driver informed them that the bus exchange would only take half an hour and then they would be on their way again. Many were confused as the schedule said that the bus should arrive at four twenty and depart at five o five, it was just four fifteen. The passengers disembarked to collect their luggage. Shouting orders was a short black man in a yellow vest, who perspired profusely. He was obviously happy to order the passengers about. Baggage could only be collected when all the bags had been offloaded. Eventually the passengers ambled forward, now hot and perspiring, to pick up their bags which were hauled into the station. Already a queue had formed for the bus to Orlando. James stuck his on the end. The other American passengers left their bags hoping they would not be removed; obviously this was standard behaviour. In Britain the bags would have been removed and possibly blown up as a security risk, here in Florida attitudes to security had not changed, despite the reassurance of the President after the happenings of 9/11. Americans still had a hard lesson to learn; that terrorism was a real threat, which sadly people in the UK had already learnt. Nevertheless James followed the crowd and left his bag and searched for the toilet. Thank goodness Marge had the foresight to give him some slices of pizza and ensured that he had a bottle of water. They had all been consumed by the time they had arrived in Tampa. He returned to stand in the line for an hour.

The official at the front of the queue gave instructions, however a foreigner, that is anyone outside Florida, would never have understood him. James was now getting used to travel officials who barked out instructions whether it be Latvians on Irish aircraft or a French ground stewardess who shouted in 'franglais', ' do you not speak English?' and Americans from the South who believe everyone can speak and understand their drawl. He followed the crowd. They shuffled forward but no one was going nowhere at five o five. They moved at five fifteen, but on which clock? There were two clocks in the station, five minutes apart. It was likely that the bus company would choose the one which would confirm that their buses ran on time.

A blind man was manoeuvred back onto the bus; he had joined the bus earlier. It was noticeable that the bus company staff showed him great care and consideration as they sat him in the front seat. They carried his entire luggage, which they then loaded onto the overhead rack which he was able to reach with ease. He wore a light brown Fedora hat and a red patterned neckerchief and carried a substantial wooden walking stick, his sun tanned face was deeply lined and he spoke with a stumbling broad southern accent. A young man wearing a green top had taken charge and made it obvious that he was going to look after this old man on his journey. At five twenty five the bus moved forward for the tourist town of Orlando, in the hands of a black lady bus driver. She began her briefing in a similar fashion found on airlines. His mind tumbled, would they soon get airborne? She abruptly stopped her drawl to tell the lady behind her to stop talking so loudly on her telephone. 'You should show consideration to other passengers', the driver shouted.....quite right. The bus turned the corner and nearly ran over two pedestrians. The bus jerked to a stop. The driver hooted the horn but the two females simply pointed to the traffic lights, it said simply WALK.

The driver continued her briefing and told the nearly full bus that this bus was to take them to Atlanta, Georgia. They would have no further bus changes and they would depart from Orlando at half past eight. He sat back relieved that the baggage would stay where it was. A quick stop was made at Lakeland so that they were soon on the outskirts of Orlando, the British holidaymaker's American paradise. Disney, Sea World, shops and fast foods were part of the popular holiday package. Lots of modern hotels and fancy restaurants sped by. James recognised the twin towers of the hotel where he used to spend ten hours rest before flying the B767 back to Manchester. In those days he was often exhausted, not knowing which side of the world he was on. Hands together he uttered a silent prayer thanking God those days were over. Rolling down 'I Drive' they arrived at the bus station in downtown Orlando.

A new bus had been ordered as yet again the air conditioning had failed on the inbound bus. A new bus arrived and all their bags were thankfully transferred automatically by the Greyhound staff. Despite that the bus left twenty minutes late. Another change of driver; he was a black driver who wore glasses and was as cheeky as the earlier ones. He was to drive us all the way to Atlanta, a long journey along the I 75 highway. Night had fallen and the lights and signs blended into one. The land was flat and boring. James became bored and began to doze; it had been a long day. He was jolted to his senses when a restricted part of the road came into view. A big flashing arrow indicated a narrowing of the lanes, with cones, orange and white stripes on the nearside lane and a long concrete wall on the outside lane. Suddenly they were upon a line of semis. They were growling and racing through the night. The driver swung out into the outside lane ready to overtake one of the juggernauts. They crept forward with inches to spare on either side. He recalled his feelings of the French film made over fifty years ago, 'Wages of fear'. The truck in the film that was carrying the dynamite was in a similar precarious position. They moved slowly forward foot by foot. The concrete wall on the left was just a passenger's arm length away. They were ahead of the truck when the driver swung back into the nearside lane, only another eight semis to go. One could see their red tail lights spread far into the distance. James was numb and silent, would this driver have the skill and alertness to pass the rest; it was getting on for half past one? They pulled out again and again and passed each vehicle in turn, quickly and safely. The passengers were full of admiration for the driver, he was good and James felt very relieved.

James moved from the window to the aisle seat, stretched his legs and as his eyelids became as heavy as hamburgers they pressed his eyes closed. He could feel the heavy breathing of a lady sitting on the inside seat. She had long dark hair, rich with a tinge of red. Was she Irish or American, a gypsy or a princess? She was stroking his hand, he nestled up, and her warm bosom caressed his cheek. He felt at peace and drifted into a deep sleep. Was she from Lochinvar or Camelot? She was the maid who served the Viscountess. She was middle aged and charming, she told him about Camelot and drifted on about the old English King who had lived in those parts and the myths related to King Arthur, not of lakes and lands far off, but in the backwoods and ponds near Gumley. In Leicestershire, deep in the heart of England was the beautiful quaint village of Gumley. It had been confiscated by the Government in the last war and used as a training village for 'the Resistance' and the SOE. The ladies' arms closed around him, he was secure; he fell enclosed into the land of dreams.

He roused, no woman but he had embraced his rucksack; the driver must have woken him when he had announced that they were just twenty minutes from Atlanta. The waning moon was shining as a very bright half dollar illuminating the flat and barren landscape; the ghosts of Yankees and Confederates marched through the night leaving the burning city. From Florida to the Atlanta outskirts everything had appeared pretty flat. He blinked, the beautiful lady had gone. He woke up stiff, slumped over the other seat, his cheek had been jammed up to the window and the curve of the seat had been digging into him. Soon the highway widened and large concrete buildings passed by. Where were the famous houses from 'Gone with the Wind'? That's what tourists came to Atlanta to see! The highway did not pass that area of the city, besides which the night mist was beginning to camouflage the tall pillared 'ante bellum' houses.

The concrete ribbon led them downtown to the bus terminal. The bus stopped in an adjacent street to the terminal where the post sleep passengers collected their bags in a quiet orderly manner. No official barking orders here, but it was about four in the morning. Pulling their cases up the ramp they saw the hand written note which said, "Entrance to the Terminal Gate", followed by a big arrow. This meant a longer dozy walk to the far gate before one could enter the hubbub. Several passengers had complimented the driver for driving them this far. It had been comforting to have a driver where one could relax and rely on as they sped through the night. He never did reveal his name; he had worn a yellow jacket which had covered his name tag.

He knew the drill and joined the long line. It had already been started by the passengers whose partners had rushed for the terminal as soon as the bus door had been opened. They were firmly positioned at the front of the queue. Our traveller was learning. By now it was five in the morning he was tired, thirsty and aching to be on his way. In a parallel queue James was interested in a fellow traveller; he was a Scotsman who lived in Tupelo, birthplace of Elvis. He began to enquire as to what he was doing there. The Glaswegian explained that he had been across to Orlando to meet his two sisters who had flown in from London. They had brought him two bulging suitcases of British goods which would have cost him a fortune to fly them onto Memphis, the nearest airport to Tupelo. This brought about his presence in the early morning Greyhound queue in Atlanta.

The clock ticked round and he crept back into the line. The young looking man in his grey blue hat and ginger hair fell backwards over his case. This alarmed James as he was just in front of him, he immediately thought like himself, the young man must have been tired. The youth gave a loud embarrassed laugh, stood up and looked around. Seconds later he launched himself, like Superman, towards a large round trash can. Others were more alert than James was, "Seizure, seizure!" some cried. One man began to clear the space around the poor man, but no official arrived. More screams to all but to no one in particular. Eventually after a few minutes, when the bus company officials had finished their chat, someone came over and attended the downed victim. Still no first aid seemed to be applied. James hid; he did not want to get involved; this was his first experience of a 'seizure' in the States. The paramedics arrived just as the passengers were called to board the bus. Shuffling forward James thought that this must be the end of the young man's journey. The paramedics told the patient to lie still whilst they did their tests. As on a previous stop a big black girl barged her way to the front of the queue. People were too tired to argue.

Climbing aboard James was lucky enough to find a double seat for himself, although the bus was now quite full. There had been another driver change. This driver was white, grey haired and noticeable by wearing a yellow tabard. The blind man was once again loaded by his young helper. The helper was about twenty five; he made sure his charge was comfortable. The driver descended from the bus. What now? More minutes ticked by. When the driver did appear he was followed by the man who had had the seizure. He moved down the bus to stop by James, he wanted to sit next to him. He left his seat so that this epileptic could sit by the window. He had obviously been passed fit to travel and had brought his oversize bag to squeeze under his seat. The bag was too big to squeeze anywhere so he had to sit with it on his lap, which overflowed onto James who was not only worried about the passenger's condition but was feeling hemmed in. The outside seat gave James an easy exit should the stranger have another fit. He noted in passing that the seat was adjacent to an emergency exit but no one seemed bothered.

The lights were switched off as they left the dramatic stop in Atlanta; they were on their way to Tennessee. No announcements but the bus lurched forward as the driver violently released the clutch. It was so sudden that James thought he had hurt his back. On the previous bus the readings lights had not worked so they had to ride in the dark; it was the same in this new bus. Thinking positively he thought it would allow people to sleep or do what they wanted to do in the dark without disturbing other passengers. Dawn would soon be breaking.

The bus drove through the well lit streets of Atlanta to the highway. It was soon stopping and a family of four, just ahead of James, disembarked. The little black children had been so good and well behaved. He moved forward into the vacated double seat. The 'seizure' man now had somewhere to put his bag and James could relax knowing that he was no longer sitting next to someone who could suddenly be sick, or violently jump on him.

Back on the I 75 with the sun beginning to lighten the day he could vaguely make out a change in the scenery. Suddenly the big green sign 'Chattanooga' roared up alongside the highway, they were in or close to the Tennessee border. They were obviously getting closer to Chattanooga but he didn't recognise it. They were closing in when he saw 'Lookout Mountain' and the surrounding hills, where was the railway station? He searched in vain. His choir in Wigston, the Male Voice Choir, had often sung a rendition of the famous song 'Chattanooga Choo Choo'. He was very disappointed not to see the edifice amongst the sprawling buildings on the right. Cutting through the deep valleys, the multitude of high green trees and the large lakes on either side of the highway he knew that he had now returned to his favourite State, Tennessee.

The sun rose and the air conditioning was working. He realised that they must have made some stops whilst he dozed. They had acquired a large black lady, who sat in front of him. She had jet black long curly hair, ball bearing dark eyes and hot red lips with a voice to match. This was 'Gloria', an ex US Army driver who had been to war in Iraq. No wonder Sadam Hussain gave himself up, she met him! Her voice became like one of those AK47s that never stopped firing. James prayed for a gun jam or a misfire. Sadly it didn't happen. The blind man who had sat on the front seat of the bus was no longer with them. The giant vehicle pulled into the town of Manchester. James doubted that anyone on the bus realised the connection between the 'Deep South', slavery and the cotton fields with the hungry consummate city of cotton in the north of England. Who had the better life, the black skinned slaves of the Mississippi or the white skinned slaves working in those 'dark satanic mills', in cold wet conditions, machinery slicing fingers and hands off? Were the people in the Deep South aware of the dependence of the cotton trade with old Manchester in the UK? This important trade had led the British Government to help finance the Confederate Army, had built fighting ships, the 'Alabama', and after the Confederate defeat in the Civil War had paid the 'Yankees' a vast sum of money in retribution fees. However many free slaves had travelled back to settle in Manchester and Liverpool in the years following the American Civil War. Nevertheless what people say, there will always be a bond between these nations, Great Britain and the United States, no matter what politicians or the media speculate, as there are so many relatives and forefathers spread across the Atlantic, we are still family.

Rolling along the highway they were soon passing the sign for the 'Jack Daniels' distillery followed by many large road side signs for motels, hotels, and restaurants inviting the world for breakfast. Pancakes, grits, eggs and sausage were up there. Stomachs turned as many were now very hungry. The reserve, bought earlier, of toast, slices of Pizza and two emergency chocolate eggs had long been eaten. A sign for Murfreesboro 30 miles ahead caught his eye. Nearly there so James began packing his bag. Off with his nightwear, shirt and pullover and on with a clean shirt. He thought about having a wash but he had had a quick shave and swill in Chattanooga. His sister Judith and husband Mike would have to take him as he was.

'Seizure, stop the bus!' They froze, James couldn't believe it! The bus began to slow but already a male passenger, across from James, had his pink mobile phone out and was dialling 911. James looked around for the man he had previously sat next to, the man who had had a seizure in Atlanta. He was crouched low in his seat. He immediately realised that it wasn't him who had collapsed. It was some poor other fellow. Gloria, the experienced truck driver ahead of him, rose up, took a deep breath with her extensive bosom and screeched that the man who was ill had had a seizure in Atlanta. James' mouthed words 'that it wasn't ', fell on deaf ears. The man who had made the initial emergency call was now saying that the collapsed man had had a fit in Atlanta. James kept silent. The bus driver pulled the bus over to the 'hard shoulder'. He secured his bus then spoke to the man with the pink phone. He asked if the caller knew where they were in order for the ambulance to find them. Adjacent to the bus door on the green verge was a large bright sign stating exactly where they were. On it was the turn off number ahead and the name of the next village, so that was easy to pass on. The driver then went to look at the patient who was lying in the aisle towards the back of the bus. James was unable to see him so could not identify him. It did not sound good from the noises coming from the rear of the bus. Several ambulances with no flashing lights passed them by. Each one was identified by the passengers screaming, 'Ambulance, ambulance', but none stopped. You had to have the correct ambulance, the one from the company you had given your order to. A State Trooper arrived, lights flashing and sirens screaming, he parked his vehicle ahead of the bus. The driver left the bus to see the official in his 'Mounties' hat. James was amazed with the action of the Trooper. He never allowed the driver to explain the situation but castigated him for stopping on the shoulder of the road. Eventually the Trooper paused for breath and the driver said his piece, immediately the trooper climbed aboard to see the casualty. Where was the driver supposed to park his bus? Eventually the ambulance arrived, a multitude of red and white flashing lights. It parked just ahead of the bus and soon disgorged two paramedics and a trolley, a gurney in American terms. They boarded the bus and were soon treating the patient. Finally they lifted him up onto his feet. James was then able to identify him as the young man with the green top who had been looking after the blind man. He felt very sorry for the young man as he had bitten his tongue and his face was covered in blood. James thought what a poor guy who was full of generosity towards the blind man, now this was his reward. He was gently handled down the bus, shaking, looking very pale. He was carefully laid on to the trolley with his belongings, and wheeled to the ambulance. James noticed that his head and hands were shaking very badly; it took him all his effort to hold onto his bag.

The ambulance sped off. The Trooper left after the driver had climbed aboard and closed the bus door. The Police car roared off down the road towards Murfreesboro. The bus pulled onto the highway; it was now running an hour and twenty minutes late. They had only driven for a few minutes when they were departing the I 75 for his destination. James just hoped his sister and husband were there. They came up the slipway and crossed the road into a garage forecourt. One could just make out the Greyhound sign. They had arrived in Murfreesboro and there were his folks waiting patiently. James disembarked, collected his luggage and thanked the driver. He was off north to places James had never heard of, except Nashville and New York. He wondered if the bus would get through the floods in Nashville.

After greeting his folks they were soon on their way, returning to their home a mile down the road. In that time he began reflecting on his ride. He had been travelling for over twenty six hours. He had had an insight into another society, another generation and had swirled around the melting pot of the United States. He had experienced travelling the Greyhound bus and wondered if he would ever do it again? Probably, but not so far next time. The buses had proved reliable, bar a few minor technical faults, air conditioning and interior lights, had safe drivers and comfortable seats. James had been able to see many parts of the South that he would normally have never seen and he had arrived safely and for that he was very grateful. The bus disappeared turning down the slipway back onto the freeway, next stop Nashville.

Bon Voyage!

The Handbag

I am sitting in the lounge of the Hotel Alma in the Rue Joy Camus. It is a fresh bright blue sunny day. Spring in Paris is such a delightful time of the year. The leaves are vibrant green, the air smells sweet and the people are going about their business in a happy mood. Opposite is the Bar des Theatres and three hundred metres away the Seine. Between here and there is the underpass where Princess Diana was killed. You and the average tourist would not know as there are no official signs. There are no memorials just a diatribe written in black marker pen on a large stone across the parapet of the bridge. A student had poured her heart out. This morning I am empty headed, I am in love and looking forward to the weekend.

'Good Morning. How is Albert this fine morning?'

It was my dear friend Arno. Arno is not Parisian, that he would soon let you know. He was born some one hundred and fifty kilometres south of Paris; a farmer's boy who came to Paris at an early age. He was now middle aged, of medium build, with dark hair, brown eyes and long slender hands. His upper lip supported a 'Poirot' moustache which completed the picture; seen in his beautiful cut of clothes he looked and smelt adorable.

Arno was the head waiter in the Bar des Theatres, the restaurant opposite the hotel. We were close friends but our secret made us even closer. He knew what really happened those years ago in the fifth quarter of Paris, although I still suffer from the memories.

'Ca va?' Arno addressed me,

'I am fine, my dear friend. Come and have a coffee before you start work.'

'Thank you, I will and I must tell you about a peculiar message I have for Justine.'

My stomach cramped up but I generated a smile; what has Arno brought me today? My mind drifted.

I had worked in the fashion industry for several years. Dior had been my latest employer and we often visited the Bar des Theatres that was just round the corner from the Dior house. Close by were many other famous names including Givenchy, YSL and Louis Vuitton. Arno had been a head waiter then, so I knew him, but I had also come to know Arno when he invited me play my classical guitar on special musical evenings in the restaurant. One evening he took me aside.

'I have recently heard two Eastern gentlemen plotting to rob Dior of a handbag. I believe Justine is taking the latest one to show in Milan, is she safe?'

'I know she departs tomorrow, perhaps I shall have to call her. She is very independent and looks after herself but with her unique aquiline nose, and those lake sized eyes she is easily identifiable,'

I called Justine but there was no reply. I left a message for her to call me then left Arno to begin my own enquiries. There was no sign of Justine. She was a metre and a half tall, striking blonde hair, had a beautiful body, but so slim it was unnatural. She was a Dior favourite. I soon had a lead. Someone had seen her being bundled into a taxi at knife point. As no one had set alarm bells ringing she must have felt abandoned. I felt desperate and realised that with my stomach churning, eyes diluting and clammy hands, I must locate her as soon as I could. I was lucky to find someone who had seen a similar taxi around the cellar entrance on the bank opposite the Eiffel Tower. Those were the same cellars where the French people had hidden their wines from the Nazis in the last war. From the description I was given I knew she was carrying that unique handbag.

I just hoped she had not been harmed for that bag, no matter how expensive it was. I began to realise the chase was not just for a handbag but also for all the unwritten and unsaid thoughts that had passed between us. That was the reason the search had become so vital. I remembered the smell of her hands; not the common cream that many of the girls in the House chose, but something else, much richer. My nostrils twitched; lemons fresh from the vine, that ardour that reminds you of crepes, gin and tonic and intimate parties. She had large mottled green eyes under long thin eyelashes that were like blinds to her mysterious mind when closed. Rich inviting lips, not botoxed and unreal but finely shaped, not razor sharp but lovable, inspiring and natural that complemented her French high cheek bones. I adored her face. I began to understand my passion for this nomadic woman, she had to be rescued and brought to my arms. I knew she would never have cheated on Dior, even though I had heard some suspicious murmurings that she could be implicated in this crime. I had to save her honour and not allow her to be harmed.

I returned to Arno and soon realised that he knew more than I first thought. Arno the waiter was more, much more; I saw the incoming tide of realisation, he slowly revealed that he was the eyes and ears of a special department in the sécurité. He had given me some vital information before he had told his department: he realised how the scandal would have affected Justine and the House of Dior. He had doubts about Justine's loyalty, he questioned me, was she was complicit in this kidnapping? I pointed out she would not risk her honour and career for a hand bag but I emphasised it was still important that I found her first. He reassured me. Arno agreed that we would keep the information to ourselves for the time being. It was in the early morning of that night we took a cab to the right bank opposite the Eiffel Tower and made our way silently towards the cellars and the dungeons. I was aware that we had been joined by several well built men, smelling of late dinner garlic but quiet as snails waiting to emerge. These were Arno's friends, the off duty sécurité, who when asked came without question. Thank goodness the air was dry and all you could hear was the occasional traffic on the road but too late for the swish of a single bateaux mouche that had earlier plied up and down the Seine on a late night dinner cruise.

We found the entrance and listened. We waited, silence, we padded down the steps. At one door it was obvious that it had been used recently, several bolts had been pulled back but the door was locked.   Arno called for silence and sure enough we heard a soft murmuring, 'Capri c'est fini'. His heavy men soon had the door opened and there by the light of the lamp we saw the crumpled shape of Justine, smaller than I imagined, cold and frightened but still humming. We soon had her untied and gently asked her if she could give us any information. Thankfully she had heard the foreigners talking. Not all the abductors were from the same country, they had conversed in French, English and Arabic.   Justine, although she was still drowsy from the ether, had been conscious enough to hear some vital clues. The handbag was to be taken to Les Invalides for an exchange at six that morning. Les Invalides, Napoleon's tomb, was not too far away. We had to assume how many would be there when the exchange took place.

We hatched a plan; the handbag had to be returned to Dior so that Justine could display it in Milan, however we were still in the dark as to who had stolen it. Our thoughts focused on who could make use of it; could it have been the brilliant forgers in Singapore? Reassured that Justine was safe I was prepared to help

Arno in any way I could. We decided to assemble at the tomb of Napoleon and survey the scene. Les Invalides was silent, cold and barren of movement on that morning in February. A cold mist clung to the trees.

We became aware of a couple of hostile figures near the high metal gates. Arno deployed his men. It only took a few seconds before they had surrounded the two tall looking guardsmen. Arno walked up to them casually and began asking them questions; one would have thought he was a tourist, lost in the early hours of the morning. We were suddenly aware that Arno and the two men had left their post and were now approaching us. I heard them talking quietly, my eyes widened, these guys were British. They were smartly dressed and spoke with an eloquent soft, British styled, French accent. They were speaking rapidly and openly. Obviously relaxed, aware their cover had been exposed they were straining to leave; they began shaking when they saw us. A black Citroen slid quietly into the market square. The British men were secured, gagged and hidden. Arno and his men discreetly crossed the square and surrounded the Citroen. Arno rapped the driver's window; it was wound down. I had no idea what was said but a handbag was passed to Arno. The car left rapidly for the Place de la Concorde.

The big dark suited guys returned to us. Arno called me over and told me the case was closed and advised me to go home and look after Justine. I drifted off with many unanswered thoughts. Where had the handbag gone?

I had seen someone dragged from the car before it left. He was interrogated and then released with the two British abductors. I still imagined Arno had a score to settle not with them but with the brains behind Justine's kidnap, but I closed my mind to further thoughts.

That was a few years ago, Justine has fully recovered and has become a well known model. I now own this hotel, thanks to a contribution from Arno, and Arno is not just the head waiter across the road, he owns the Bar de Theatres.

'By the way Arno what was the mysterious message for Justine?'

'Oh! I was contacted by that well known fashion house in London, they wanted to return a favour and have offered your wife Justine, a contract that she will not refuse. They said it was a bag for a bag and she would understand.'

A gentle smile crossed his face. I thought back to the Milan show, Justine had appeared late with that handbag. I often wondered where it had come from. Nobody mentioned the delay. Was Arno kidding? I sighed, slid on my jacket and left to collect a couple of tickets for London.

               *   *   *

You can still meet Arno today, working hard in the restaurant of the Bar de Theatre; he will never admit his 'other job'. We met him the weekend of the Paris Marathon; we were supporting Rich George and Duncs Clarke for their pounding around Paris. It was a bit chaotic, but that's another tale. Enjoy the food and wine at the Bar de Theatre but my advice is - keep your eye on your handbag!

A Beach in Keri Keri, New Zealand

The Lookout

The clock struck four; it was the Westminster chime, loud in the still of night. It was the first time David had heard it; he rolled out of bed and made for the kitchen. He had just flown in from London with a stop in Hong Kong. He was sleepy but needed a drink, his throat was bone dry.

His eye twitched, he shuffled to the kitchen. He noticed his shaky finger nails, smooth and rounded. His breathing was as tight as the rubber line tied tight in a golf ball. A good swing and he would have fallen. The reflection in the mirror was of a white tram - lined gaunt face. Where was the vibrant young man of yesteryear? Houdini would be needed to release the chains that bound him and free his spirit. He could smell his dark dank sweaty skin. He was glad for this break and the release from the business he had left, the years has passed, he had retired.

The flight had been long but the shower and the massage in Hong Kong had passed the time before boarding the flight for Auckland. The shower had been refreshing; the massage excruciating; he ached all over. He was overweight for his medium height; the seat had been too tight. Approaching Auckland he had great difficulty in getting his shoes back on; the steward kindly explained that it was due to the cabin air pressure that his feet had swollen. Fortunately the flight to the Bay of Islands left on schedule despite the terrible weather. They had cancelled all flights to KeriKeri that morning, so once again he was subject to a full flight and a heaving mass of passengers: so tightly cramped they breathed in and out with a spectacular rhythm. Descending into low clouds and slashing rain, sliding sideways, a couple of bumps and the pilot had greased the elegant craft onto the plain of KeriKeri.

The house in Reinga Road was hidden in exotic trees and plants. It had several rooms surrounded by sliding glass doors that looked across the decking to a panoramic vista which was the Bay of Islands and the vast inlet which led into the old harbour at Stone Store. That solid grey structure was the oldest building in New Zealand and on its lawn Maoris had eaten the white worshiping Christian ministry, limb by limb. That was a long time ago and things had changed but the Stone Store stood unchallenged.

The decking, surrounding the house, was guarded by a green railing which saved one from tumbling into the green drop of multifarious coloured tropical plants some feet below, and below that the azure long clear cool water of the swimming pool. Kept to a luke warm temperature, surrounded by green bushes, swaying and smelling of fresh tropical fruits it drew one down, into nakedness, to plunge into the delights of a large warm bath. The rain ran down the deck, spitting and throbbing, reducing as the clock ticked on. The dark heavy mist enclosed the inky inlet with only a sharp glimpse of water. The soft sticky mist drifted revealing slakes of mud. The tide was coming in.

Further up the hill is the old Maori 'lookout' post for the bay, not as big as a pa, a Maori fort, but recognised as such by the countless number of shells found at the top of the hill. It was a corner of a kingdom that was once held by Hone Heke, a warrior Maori tribal chief. He had led a powerful, war mongering tribe. The Haka did little justice to the fear it brought to his enemies. However he did make an agreement in 1840 with the English, from Sydney, that they would defend the Maoris against an expected French invasion of Northland.

As David settled into a comfortable armchair, the veil of flowing mist was lifting, hypnotically he watched as an old two masted ketch drift eerily towards the coastline. He saw that it was crewed by a few dark figures, swarthy, muscular with dark heads of hair. He heard not a sound but the ship moved closer. The mist looked lighter over the water, flat, still like a pond. The only thing he could see besides the boat was the outline of a black log peeping out of the water; that log had been there for years.

The ketch was the type that had harboured in Russell Island in the 1840's. Two tall masts, cloaked by a heavy quilt which languidly drifted forming a bubblegum balloon, billowing. It was tied to the ship by a spider's golden thread. It drew closer.

The sails flapped and ropes moved over their pulleys, the bow of the ship was now pointing towards the revealing jetty. On the jetty were three distinct shapes, two standing and one sitting. The one sitting was astride a dark brown coffin. The coffin was big, wide and long, Maori sized. The rest of the jetty was deserted. The boat bumped the jetty, it was quickly lashed to a stanchion, swiftly and silently the three men slid the large coffin aboard. It was placed gently on the foredeck then the sailors lashed it securely. Two men boarded whilst the third cast off and helped the prow move round into deeper water. He crossed the stern and embarked as it passed. The ketch slowly, very slowly moved out to face the dark cave from whence it came. The rolling mist, as on cue began to envelope the sails, first one and then the other tall mast, followed by the body of the ship. It was gone into the night.

No ghost from the 'lookout' had seen the ship. David rubbed his eyes; rain fell again splattering on the deck and began drumming like a kettle drum. Gradually slithers of silvery water began breaking through the now translucent mist.

The clock chimed six bells and all was well: his heavy eyes closed.

Later in the day David rose to a bright January morning. The water was alive with light, bouncing off the full tide which had flooded the inlet. The jet lag had caught up with him; he dozed turning over in his mind the dream he had had, or had he? He eventually crept into the spacious lounge, walked out onto the deck. He glanced across the busy inlet which stretched from left to right. He could see half a dozen swing poles which sat in the deeper part, opposite the big houses. They were moorings for sailors. He wondered if he could confirm what he had seen in the night. No ketch, a full inlet of water, the log, but no jetty, such are the Maori spells in these parts: he pondered.

Sometime later on, it was pointed out that there were several Maori homes on the other side of the inlet. They had a Marae, their meeting place, and a cemetery. Funerals were big business. When a funeral took place one would see a multitude of mourning Maoris; they had large extended families. He also learnt that much further across the inlet, in the cleft of the hill, was a large red roofed house that belonged to Michael Crawford; the famous television and light opera star. His mind tumbled; if Crawford's presence had much influence then, despite the Maoris, 'the Phantom' would be casting a different spell.

Hypothermia Hubris

A tale of woe is laid before, for you to judge but ask no more

Of honest men who risk it all, to keep a friendship

Strong winds still blew from the Antarctic Sea
To New Zealand's South Isle so icily
Just Christmas past, some friends they came
To see Lindsay Cullens, and with no shame
asked to go fishing in the Strait, but he
had no boat so asked his mate

His friend for life was Barry Bethune
great families, whanau, together in tune.
It was still summer in those South Seas
so despite the weather, sharp on the run, took
Barry's paua vessel with Shaun his son
Who left his family, to help his Dad
Best of mates and fishing mad!

The Kiwis known for strength and grit
The sea was their heaven and knowing it
had abundant fish, but alas sharp winds it took
their rods and lines and all their hooks
A crashing wave whipped up the boat
Left Lindsay's head both crushed and broke

Thrown from the boat into the inky sea
His circle made, Shaun swam strong, silently
White Island passed, it was so near
Currents ran fast but he showed no fear
Shaun was drained and cold was he
Then drifted off with mate Lindsey
His friend of old, they quietly, disappeared.

Now Shaun's Dad was all but spent
When on the far distant beach, a tent
Slept a couple who saw their plight
Ergo the Maori launched, into the night.
But his small craft it could not hold
the three survivors. He then swiftly told
them, 'Don't come aboard, just hold real tight'
Then rowed and rowed with all his might

The virile pull, the current strong
So to the shore, it was not long
Now desolate Barry has time to reflect
On family and friends but Oh! Sore regret
What price was paid for his son Shaun?

His kindness he knows, will ever be borne
Now Uncle Pete, his name well known
said these few words of his nephew Shaun
'Tough little bastard', was his plaintive plea
But toughness alone will not conquer the sea

The Maoris they know from sayings of old
That currents do, we are often told,
Bind tides with waves that forever, ebb and flow
Those self-same currents that rise from the deep
Bind all of us people when or wherever we sleep.

Maori Words

Paua = Abalone shell, pronounced 'power'

Whanau = Family, pronounced 'fano'

This is a poem dedicated to the people who died that night and to the rescuer. Sadly some months later the rescuer himself was out fishing and he himself was caught in difficulties by atrocious weather. He drowned leaving a widow.

Such are the vagaries of the Southern Ocean and the waters of the South Island in New Zealand. The sea is a sacred part of the Maori culture.

The Dinner: Borres

In the centre of France, just a bit north of the Dordogne River is the small village of Borres. Climb the hill leading out to the north and there on the side of the road are two large white stones, carved in Times New Roman are the words, 'Pierre Dorres'.

They had abandoned their cars at the bottom of the hill. Slowly in the searing late June sun they were now climbing the hill along the narrow winding lane, looking for the stone which was inscribed 'Pierre Dorres'. Sweat was trickling down arms and legs. The drive had been a long one from Leicestershire to the Dordogne. The two families had become good friends thanks to an association with the charity organisation, Round Table. The parents had cemented their relationship at a very jovial dinner in Hinckley some years previously. This was to be a big family holiday; it was going to be three weeks of togetherness.

The cars were reliable and the journey straightforward but they had to drive on the right, negotiate French traffic and rely on the front seat passenger's judgement for the overtaking gaps. Nobody had been killed or injured but nerves had been jangled. They had come to stay in Wally and Doreen's place. The two families were now exhausted.

Doreen was an ex-headmistress from St. Trinians'. Not really, but you could have imagined that she had been, bossy, beautiful and great fun. A lady, who would never grow old, medium built, married to a calm and sophisticated husband, Wally. He was a handsome six foot chap, who not only played cricket for a local team, but managed in broken French to conduct a French choir. Doreen had been running camping sites in her school summer holidays when she decided Wally was working too hard as a manager in Maidstone, Kent and should move to France permanently. They bought the large house, 'Pierre Dorres' and Wally with great skill and fortitude had transformed the building into three houses, one of which became their home. Grey walled, solid block and two stories high it was imposing, with a large garden, in the centre of which was a large azure, sequined sparkling inviting swimming pool. Flowers of bright vivid colours surrounded the pool and the house; an idyllic spot in a quiet valley.

The Georges; Helen, Steve, Justine, Justine's bestest friend Jo Hutch, Richard and Granny Pauline, had the centre house. The Poddy's; Ann, Mike, Claire and her friend Darren had the end house. They quickly settled in and were soon relaxing by the large pool. Mike worked for Coventry Council but his talent, with Ann, was raising loads of money for charity. He should have written a book on how to do it and sold it to raise more cash. Ann was just a brilliant cook who had cooked for so many including the Glenn Miller Band, led by Glenn's nephew, John. They had played a couple of concerts for their Round Table in the 80's.Again they raised thousands and made a lot of people happy. Helen taught French at a secondary school, so the party had a holiday interpreter. The children were at various schools.

'Help, help!' the screams from the end house shattered the silence.

Ann was cowered in the corner of the top house, as the fretful bat swooped around the room. They all crowded in causing the bat to increase the frequency of swoops. Helen grabbed a stick and as the bat escaped the room and burrowed into the ivy surrounding the door, she thrashed the plant. Eventually the poor bat escaped and flew away. It was an excuse to relax and enjoy the opportunity of sampling the local wine. Welcome to la Belle France.

The area had been a hive for the French resistance. Just down the road, about three kilometres away was a cross road which was commemorated as a place of an ambush against the Germans during the last World War. In a local village there was a plaque on the large wall in the centre stating that it was the place where many men women and children had been executed by the Nazis. The large viaduct on the way to Souillac had been blown up in June 1944 to prevent reinforcements rushing from the Dordogne to Normandy. It was destroyed by the efforts of the Americans in SOE and by the Resistance. The Americans had warned the local populace to keep their windows open on the night of the raid, thus saving all their windows! Coincidentally the SOE had taken off from a secret airbase close to the Leicestershire border at Harrington. It was this SOE group that had first carried and used the 'S' phone which when developed, invaded the whole world from the 1960's as the mobile phone. One sensed the local people's dislike for Germans and few German tourists were seen in the area.

July came and the centre of the village became a centre for noisy activity. A marquee was constructed and the dance floor laid. Excitement grew as the 14th of July approached, Bastille Day. The night was a party night where locals and tourists joined together to celebrate the national holiday. Wine, beer and Orangina was drunk by the bottle, music blasted out and the centre was a glow of bright colours and pulsating feet. Children generated their energy into the adults and even the grumpy old men grabbed who they could and drifted around the floor. The night went on and on. People began to drift away, teenagers were still left in small groups but by midnight the adults were slowly climbing the steep hills to their welcome beds.

The next day even the birds were slow to cheep, the sun rose slowly and a mist covered the valley. Today Angela and Vince Hutchinson would be coming to see their daughter Jo. They had been in Spain and were travelling back home to Cadeby, a sleepy village in the heart of England. They arrived, happy suntanned and ready for a spot of lunch followed by a few days of relaxation. However Jo and Justine were still sore headed, deep in their beds, sleeping off the revelries of the previous night. The girls were roused and lunch was begun. Over lunch it was decided to ask 'les Patrons' if they could arrange a meal at the local restaurant that evening. Doreen was approached, she quite sensibly pointed out it was the night after 'La Bastille', and a large dinner may be difficult to arrange. The decision was made; they pressed on.

Three families with their sponsors assembled at the top of the hill and made their way down to the village restaurant. It was a moving murmur punctuated by giggles from the girls. Once inside the restaurant the three families were placed at the top table. On either side were two long tables where a variety of nationals were sitting. Dutch, Irish, French and a family from Birmingham, they spoke English but differently, a language based on Dudley Anglo Saxon Olde English!

The waiter, bleary eyed brought on the menu. Soup, fresh trout fish or locally free range chicken.

'I think we ought to recognise the French celebration so please stand and we shall all sing La Marseilles'; Doreen had grabbed the mood. Chairs were pushed back with scraping and puffing as people rose to sing the French National Anthem. All the diners, adults and children stood in deference to the French. Off they went giving their all to the rousing anthem. To their delight and surprise the French men in the bar came through the door to join them in the dining room and sang with gusto. What a start to their evening!

They ordered and waited drinking their way through the first bottles of wine. The soup was served along with many baskets of sliced baguettes. They waited, and waited for the main meal. The party had arrived at seven and it was already eight thirty. Doreen went off to investigate. She reported that there were not enough fish or pieces of chicken for all the guests so the chef had been dispatched to get fish from the fish farm and a few more chickens from the local farm. Something was needed to fill the gap before the guests became restless. Fortunately or unfortunately, depending on your taste in music, Steve had brought his guitar. He sang a couple of solo songs then suggested that each table gave a rendering. There was such a variety of national songs: it was very entertaining. Songs were then sung that all the people knew so 'The Beatles' were belted out by all. It was then noted that the people from the bar had augmented the diners and then someone saw 'le Chef'. He was singing his heart out. No wonder the fish and chicken were late in arriving on the plate! The noise grew; more songs, louder conversation and cheers when any food arrived. No one noticed how the time rolled round but finally the coffee had been served and it was time to climb the hill. They were all grateful to le Patron and le Chef but particularly to Doreen and Wally for fixing the meal.

You can still see the restaurant today tucked in the main street of Borres. Speak about the dinner after the Bastille night and the locals will still recall the night of the singing diners and the wayward chef who spent more time singing in the dining room than cooking in the kitchen. It was a moment in time to sear in the memory for ever.